INVESTING FOR TAKE-OFF

Growth to Sky-is-the-Limit

Feliciano Bantilan

Text copyright © 2014 Feliciano Bantilan
All Rights Reserved
ISBN-13: 978-1503229716
ISBN-10: 1503229718

Limit of Liability/Disclaimer of Warranty:

While the author and the publisher have used their best efforts in preparing this book, they make no representations or warranties with respect to the accuracy or completeness of the contents of this book and specifically disclaim any implied warranties of merchantability or fitness for a particular purpose. The advice and strategies contained herein may not be suitable for your situation. You should consult with a professional where appropriate. Neither the author nor the publisher shall be liable for any loss of profit or any other commercial damages, including but not limited to special, incidental, consequential, or other damages.

Dedication

To individuals contemplating to invest in the stock market:

The difference between ordinary people and the super-rich is one of thought – the super-rich believe they can grow their money, with money begetting money, while ordinary people do not even think of that possibility. Ordinary people think only of working for money. They do not think of money working for them.

Acknowledgment

My thanks go to Enrique Yaptenco for my photo on the back cover.

I appreciate the suggestion from my wife, Cynthia, for the beautiful front cover image. I am grateful for her love and support. She has been an anchor in my life. To her, go my eternal love and gratitude.

Table of Contents

Acknowledgment 5
Preface 8
    New Way of Investing 8
    Psychological Impossibility Barrier 9
Plan of Book 10
Prologue 12
Introduction: Shift in Psychology 17
    Go with the Flow 17
    Go-with-the-flow Psychology 19
Chapter 1: The Basis –Stock Market Theory 20
    Postulates and Some Consequences 21
    Random and Causal Force 24
    Causality Dominates Randomness 27
    The Arrow and the Hoisting Crane 28
Chapter 2: Before Take-off 35
    The Two Forces: Randomness and Causality 35
    Randomness and Human Nature 38
    Causality and Human Nature 46
    Go-with-the-Flow Psychology 48
Chapter 3: Take-off to Sky-is-the-Limit 54
    The Two Forces: Randomness and Causality 54
    Randomness and Human Nature 56
    Causality and Human Nature 57
    Bear Markets 59
    Go-with-the-Flow Psychology 61
Chapter 4: How Best to Ride the Causal Force 63

- Populating our Portfolio 63
- Mr Market and Stock Prices 65
- Go-with-the-Flow Psychology 68

Chapter 5: Putting Theory into Practice 70
- Passive and Active Investors 70
- First Stage: Taxi on the Runway 87
- Second Stage: Take-off to Unlimited Growth 88
- Disarming Fears of Bear Markets 89
- Retirement 93

Conclusion 96
Appendix 98
- Visualizing Portfolio Return 98

About the Author 102
- Other books by the author 103

Preface

"Almost all new ideas have a certain aspect of foolishness when they are first produced."

Alfred North Whitehead

The book presents a new way of seeing – and thus, of doing – investing in the stock market.

The theory expounded in our previous book, "Portfolio Take-off: Stock Market Theory", explained the overall behaviour of the stock market in terms of the innate dynamics of the forces – randomness and causality – driving it. The random force is a buy or a sell of shares of stocks, sending the price up or the price down. The causal force is a net-buy of shares of stocks over a period, sending the price up.

The theory predicted the existence of a portfolio take-off to unlimited growth, directly arising from the natural dynamics of the two driving forces. The prediction is borne out by an analysis of the S&P 500 index returns, from 1928 to 2013, giving an estimate of the time from the start to take-off of about 15 years.

New Way of Investing

This book spells out the implications of the theory described above on investing, generating a new way of doing investing in the stock market: the **go-with-the-flow psychology**. The key implication is that now we know our portfolio, if managed properly (minimal intervention), will take-off to unlimited growth in about 15 years – thanks to the natural flow of the driving forces in the stock market.

If we just let the innate dynamics of the driving forces take their course, then our portfolio naturally crosses the threshold into the zone of unlimited growth. This is the reality, predicted by our portfolio take-off theory, and the basis of our new way of investing. We will see that investing is what we do not do, as much as what we do.

This approach contrasts sharply from the "interventionist" way of investing – the default among many investors – resulting in much churning in our portfolio, consequently suffering from underperformance with respect to a benchmark. As Warren Buffett wryly remarked, "For investors as a whole, returns decrease as motion increases".

Psychological Impossibility Barrier

We compare the likely effect this knowledge of the "natural portfolio take-off to unlimited growth" will have on investors, to the effect on runners who came to know of the sub-4-minute-mile run by Roger Bannister on May 6, 1954. After knowing Bannister broke through the barrier, other runners too broke through the barrier of the sub-4-minute-mile run.

It was not an issue of physiology, but of psychology. Because of Bannister's achievement, the psychological impossibility barrier of a sub-4-minute-mile run fell off.

In a similar way, we expect the psychological impossibility barrier of attaining portfolio take-off to unlimited growth will also fall off. Investors will no longer think that only the likes of Warren Buffett are capable of such a feat. If they were unaware of portfolio take-off to unlimited growth before, now they are – and therefore, are aiming to achieve it. Now, the psychology is "I can do it, too". Expect many more investors will attain the "Grail" of investing – reaching the "promised land" of unlimited growth, in about 15 years from now.

Plan of Book

"One's mind, once stretched by a new idea, never regains its original dimensions."
Oliver Wendell Holmes

The Prologue starts the discussion by giving an overview of investing that naturally flows from our portfolio take-off theory and of the go-with-the-flow psychology, equally implied by the theory.

The Introduction presents the shift in our thinking, explaining the *go-with-the-flow* psychology as exemplified by a tender seedling growing in our garden, and by the effective yet graceful motion in Asian martial arts.

Chapter 1 gives the background to the development in the rest of the book, summarizing the key result and ideas of our portfolio take-off theory.

Chapter 2 discusses the first stage in the lifetime of our portfolio. The factors in focus are the dynamics of the driving forces – randomness and causality, our role bringing along with us the weaknesses of human nature, and the go-with-the-flow psychology applied to investing issues specific to the first stage.

Chapter 3, similar in structure to chapter 2, applies the same considerations to the second stage. The marked change in the disposition of the two forces signals a corresponding change in our attitude and actions.

Chapter 4 focuses on the positive action we have to take to ride best the causal force. The positive action is choosing the stocks populating our portfolio, based on the principles of Graham and Buffett. In contrast, we sidestep the random force, by inaction.

Chapter 5 rounds out our theory by putting it into practice. We go through "virtual" investing with specific recommendations for actions, simulating the important steps from the opening of a brokerage account, to what to do when a bear market comes – especially when it coincides with our retirement.

The Conclusion reinforces the idea that we ordinary individual investors can do what the rich people have done – to grow our money without limit.

The Appendix describes a way of visualizing portfolio return. Visual images aid our understanding. In particular, two agents or characters – the snail and the monkey – representing groups of processes help us visualize our portfolio return.

Prologue

"The new idea either finds a champion or it dies. No ordinary involvement with a new idea provides the energy required to cope with the indifference and resistance that change provokes."

Tom Peters

An eagle soaring in the sky uses the flow of air currents to stay aloft, gliding with grace, while riding the air.

Investing in the stock market is like the soaring of an eagle in the sky, using the force flows driving the stock market, sidestepping the negative force of randomness, while riding the positive force of causality, to reach the "Grail" of investing – **portfolio take-off to sky-is-the-limit.**

The random force is a buy or a sell of shares of stocks, sending the price up or the price down. The causal force is a net-buy of shares of stocks over a period, sending the price up.

As serious investors, we aim to grow our money; to reach our aim our portfolio needs to take-off to unlimited growth. The causal force during the first stage in the lifetime of our portfolio, builds-up its contribution to our return, while the random force is stirring up our primal emotions, sowing confusion and instigating frustration – by the fluctuations it causes in our return.

The first stage lasts for about 15 years. Then, the inevitable happens in the second stage. The single-sign contributions from the causal force result in the stacking up of return increments. On the other hand, the dual-sign contributions from the random force result in the cancellation of return increments. Thus, dictated by the innate dynamics of the two forces, the return arising from the causal force starts to pull away from that of the random force. At this point, our portfolio starts its ascent to the sky-is-the-limit.

Above is a general picture of investing for take-off guided by the go-with-the-flow psychology. We now go into some details.

The flow dynamics of the two driving forces determine our investing attitude and actions. Randomness plays a negative role in our return, while causality plays a positive one. Consequently, we have two main actions to take – one, a positive action, optimally riding the causal force; and two a negative action, sidestepping the random force.

To ride the causal force optimally, as we will show, we populate our portfolio with stocks chosen according to the two principles of sound investing – one, Graham's principle of margin of safety and two, Buffett's principle of buying good companies at below average prices. On the other hand, we sidestep the random force by doing nothing in response to return fluctuations.

The two actions described above follow the way of the martial arts as practised in Asia – not to oppose the forces, but instead to go-with-the-flow, or take advantage of the force flows. The eagle uses the same principle to ride the air currents in the sky.

The random force and the causal force, following their innate dynamics, behave distinctly in the two lifetime stages of our portfolio. In fact, the two-stage division precisely rests on the distinct force flow dynamics in each stage.

In particular, the random force, in the first stage, before take-off, plays two roles: one, it causes our return to fluctuate, what otherwise is an upward rising return; and two, it preys on the weaknesses in our psychology. In the second role, it exposes the traits of our human nature, rendering us mal-adapted to investing.

By a throw of dice, the random force frustrates our expectations, anticipating that the advance of our return in a day to hold or continue, only to find it nullified by a bigger retreat in the following day. The alternating "red" and "green" in our portfolio is its handiwork. Due to our lack of intuitive grasp of statistical processes, we mistake these fluctuations for the reality of our return. We did not inherit an iota of statistical reasoning from our ancestors in the savannahs in Africa.

Besides what it does to our return, the random force works on our psychology, sowing anxiety, fear, and sometimes-hysteric reactions among us investors, during a bear market. Great harm it does to our portfolio – not in what it does directly to our return, but in what it does indirectly via our psychology.

It is our action – coming from our psychology goaded by return fluctuations due to randomness – that actually does the damage. If we let the fluctuations of our return be, then our portfolio will be just fine – in fact, that is the best situation.

In the second stage, randomness is without real power; the only power it has arises from our psychological weakness. Yet, in spite of no real power to affect our return significantly, great harm it can still do, most especially during a massive sell-off.

Fortunately, for us, the random force has an inner flaw that eventually spells its end to insignificance, in terms of what it does to our return. However, as we will see, its hold on our psychology, in spite of wielding no more real power over our return, continues.

The causal force, on the other hand, plays a positive role in our return. It pushes our return upward to counter the downward pull from randomness. Sometimes, the random force overpowers it by sending our cumulative return underwater, below 100% - meaning we are losing a fraction of our initial capital.

In the first stage, causality plays "defence" most of the time. Its fight with randomness is about even. For about 15 years, it defends our portfolio from attacks from randomness. In the second stage, its strategy shifts to playing "offense". With its inherent strength of only positive-sign contributions to our return, the causal force builds its dominance over randomness in the second stage.

Causality carries our portfolio across the first stage to the threshold of take-off and on to the "promised" land of unlimited growth. It relentlessly continues to pull away from randomness reaching a point such that no fluctuations even bear market fluctuations can bring down the cumulative return of our portfolio to below 100%. At this point, the most that randomness can do is carve a "dimple" in our cumulative return curve, which continues to grow even higher than the peak before the bear market.

At a certain point in the second stage, a qualitative change occurs in the curve of our return – from linear to exponential. What otherwise is an exponential curve, the random force straightens to a line during the first stage. Our portfolio, in the language of Physics, reaches criticality. Just like fissile plutonium sphere, when squeezed by an imploding lens of explosives wrapped around it, crosses the threshold to criticality into a self-sustaining chain-reaction, so our portfolio after a wait of about 15 years is now in a self-sustaining money-creation chain-reaction, generating money – in principle without limit.

A chain reaction is a process in which a trigger, like a neutron breaking up a nucleus of an atom, increases in number or in size at each succeeding phase, thereby producing a self-sustaining chain reaction – a runaway process. In the stock market, the "trigger" is the amount of money in our portfolio that increases with time, triggering or begetting more money as time progresses.

In resume, investing is dealing with the two forces – randomness and causality – driving the stock market. At the same time, investing is equally dealing with our human nature reacting to the two forces.

Such briefly is the *go-with-the-flow psychology of investing for take-off*.

Investing for take-off, as well as the *go-with-the-flow psychology*, is agnostic with respect to the investing approach we choose. Whatever investing approach we use – be it the Warren Buffett buy-and-hold approach, the Ken Fisher approach, or the Phil Town approach, or the Greenblatt approach, etc. – the go-with-the-flow psychology of investing-for-take-off will improve our chances of success.

Introduction: Shift in Psychology

"Let things flow naturally forward in whatever way they like".
Lao Tzu

The random nature of the tens of millions of buy-and-sell transactions renders tracking the impact of each transaction on our return impossible. Yet, we can track the overall trajectory of the stock market return over time. This result we showed in our previous book, "Portfolio Take-off: Stock Market Theory".

Go with the Flow

The portfolio take-off theory has important implications on investing in the stock market. The overall change that the theory implies is in our psychology – our attitude toward the stock market – that natural timescales govern its random and causal processes, as expressed by its return. As shown in the book already cited, the two forces – randomness and causality – driving the stock market have their own innate dynamics.

We cannot fight the random force. If we do, we are on the losing side, as many investors are in, unknowingly. Nobody can beat the random force. We can only let it take its course. We can and should ride the causal force. For, the causal force grows our money. We can fiddle with the causal force to a certain extent to speed up the ride. Over all, though, the driving forces have each an innate dynamic that flows irrespective of what we do.

In other words, the shift in our psychology is toward a conformal attitude to the forces driving the stock market, i.e. going with their flow dynamics.

Growing a seedling

The image of a tender seedling pushing to grow in our garden is an apt image to illustrate the change induced by our theory to one of conformal attitude. We cannot grow a tree in opposition to its nature. We can grow a tree only in conformity with its nature.

The push to grow our money in the stock market is similar to the push to grow a seedling in our garden.

DNA pushes the seedling to grow. However, arrayed against its growth are the random forces, in particular, the second law of thermodynamics of disorder increase. The seedling sidesteps the second law, by unloading to the environment, a disorder increase greater than the disorder decrease it uses internally to feed its growth, thereby satisfying the second law of disorder increase.

On the other hand, our desire to provision our future pushes our money to grow. However, ranged against its growth are random forces pulling in the opposite direction. Similarly, we sidestep the random forces by ignoring them completely – a most difficult task to do for the offspring of the African savannah dwellers.

As a seedling successfully negotiates crossing the threshold of viability and on to full maturity, we too can successfully navigate the 15-year taxi-time on the runway, crossing the threshold to the portfolio take-off point and on to the zone of unlimited growth.

Motion in Martial Arts

The effective yet graceful motion in the martial arts as practised in Asia is another way of showing the shift in our psychology implied by our theory. "Do not meet force with force, but channel the force flow from your foe to throw your foe off-balance", so goes a maxim in Asian martial arts. Such mind-set is the way we should handle our investment – know the flow of the driving forces in the stock market and exploit their strength.

Go-with-the-flow Psychology

Our portfolio take-off theory induces us to adopt the new ***go-with-the-flow psychology*** of investing. Our theory tells us to let the force flows take their natural course. The current flow from randomness naturally subsides, while the current flow from causality naturally swells, in a time of about 15 years. Going-with-the-flow psychology means we exploit the strength from the force flows – we let the random force flow subside to diminution, while we ride the causal force flow that swells to domination.

The *go-with-the-flow psychology* absolutely needs patience. We patiently wait for an opening when our foe exposes vulnerability – and that is when we strike. We do not waste time, flailing at our foe. In the stock market, this means a patient wait for about 15 years.

The book explores in detail how to put the new way of investing into practice: the *go-with-the-flow psychology of investing for take-off.*

Chapter 1: The Basis –Stock Market Theory

"Daring ideas are like chessmen moved forward: they may be beaten, but they may start a winning game."

Goethe

As a background to all subsequent discussions, this chapter presents a summary of the main concepts of our portfolio take-off theory. For details, see our previous book, "Portfolio Take-off: Stock Market Theory".

The important result from the theory is the *existence of portfolio take-off to unlimited growth*. We arrived at this conclusion by analysing the natural dynamics of the forces driving the stock market. The arguments were general, without reference to specific stock markets or specific conditions.

Consequently, the conclusion, we believe, holds in all stock markets, across times and geographies. The last statement ultimately rests on the sameness of human nature, across the ages and locations.

The theoretical prediction of the existence of portfolio take-off to unlimited growth, finds empirical support from the analysis of the S&P 500 index returns, from 1928 to 2013. Using the worst patch of time in the 86-year period, the S&P 500 index took-off to unlimited growth in about 15 years, starting in 1928.

We take 15 years as our ballpark figure of the time it takes for a portfolio to take-off to unlimited growth.

We now go into some details of the elements of the theory – the postulates and their consequences, the two forces driving the stock market, randomness and causality, the argument for the winning force over time, and the handy metaphor of the *arrow and the hoisting-crane* – in preparation for the development in the rest of the book.

Postulates and Some Consequences

We get a quick sense of the portfolio take-off theory by examining its postulates, taking as it were a glance at the whole theory at once.

The Postulates of the Theory

1. Portfolio return is a composite: a random and a causal component.

Two forces drive the stock market return – one, randomness and two, causality. The random force is a buy or a sell of shares of stocks, sending the return up or the return down. The causal force is a net-buy of shares of stocks over a period, sending the return up. They act on return simultaneously, resulting in a composite behaviour of return, from the random return push-up or the random return pull-down, and from the causal return push-up. This postulate is the key starting assumption of our theory.

Portfolio return exhibits behaviours we identify as arising from randomness and causality. For instance, a plot of one-year returns of the S&P 500 index shows columns above and below the zero-return line – here, we deduce randomness at work. We notice too that there are more columns and longer above than below the zero-return line – here, we see the signature of causality.

Thus, the postulate of composite return simultaneously executing random and causal motion is eminently plausible. The issues here will find further elaboration in the section on "Random and Causal Force" below.

2. All observed behaviour of share prices that influence portfolio return springs from the buy-and-sell transactions.

The price-rise and the price-fall of shares of stocks come from the buy-and-sell transactions. We will detail the mechanism for the rise and fall of prices below.

3. The random component of return arises from the un-coordinated executions of buy-and-sell transactions, by tens of millions of investors.

The random component of return is easy to see. The buy-and-sell transactions have a random distribution, in time and in amounts. Randomness comes mainly from the short-term sentiments of investors – "hot" or "cold" toward shares of stocks – that prod them to buy or sell stocks. Further consideration is in the section on "Random and Causal Force" below.

4. The causal component of return comes from the net-buy over the long term, by investors anticipating share-price appreciation, based on the expected continuing economic growth worldwide.

Over the long term, for a given portfolio of stocks, the price-rise due to buying is greater than the price-fall due to selling. We call this a **net-buy**. In fact, in the long history of the stock market, about two thirds of the time the market has been up. More discussion is in the section on "Random and Causal Force".

5. The change in return coming from the random component can be positive or negative; consequently, the cumulative sum of return changes arising from randomness does not grow with time because of cancellation: it is zero.

The random contribution to the return is both positive – the return push-up, and negative – the return pull-down. This key feature explains the progressive diminution in influence of the random force on return over time, in contrast to the increasing domination in influence of the causal force with time. More on postulate 5 is in the section on "Causality Dominates Randomness".

6. The change in return arising from the causal component is positive; consequently, in the absence of cancellation, the cumulative sum of return changes arising from causality, boosted by compound growth effect, grows with time without limit.

The sign of the contribution of the causal force to the return is only positive – the return push-ups. This fact is the reason why stock market returns always rise over the long term. More on Postulate 6 is in the section on "Causality Dominates Randomness".

Some Consequences from the Postulates

We highlight a few consequences from the six postulates, to have a quick sense of the implications of the theory on which the rest of the book depends.

1. Directly, from postulate five and six, there must be a time when causality's contribution to return starts to pull away from that of randomness, growing the return with time without limit. We call this time the portfolio take-off time to unlimited growth.

2. The whole point of investing in stocks is to achieve take-off.

3. The length of the take-off time is beyond deduction from the postulates. Stock market return data can yield an estimate: it is about 15 years.

4. Our theory through postulate 4, gives a framework for choosing the investing approach, among the many viable approaches. There is only one criterion for the candidate approach to meet: which of the viable approaches best rides the causal force?

5. Consequence 3 shows the long-time nature of investment in the stock market. Investors should disabuse their minds of the

quick-rich myths surrounding stock investing: the sooner, the better for their portfolio.

Having taken a quick overview of our portfolio take-off theory, we move on to the two-force-component model of return, the central idea of the theory.

Random and Causal Force

Randomness and causality are ubiquitous – from the fateful encounter of pairs of microscopic eggs that eventually became us, to the spontaneous growth of weather patterns, to the seeming chaotic gyrations of stock market returns.

We briefly present in this section the contending roles of the two forces in the stock market.

The Random Force

The random force drives our portfolio return – pushing the return up, or pulling the return down. The uncoordinated buy-and-sell transactions by tens of millions of investors worldwide, at different times, in varying amounts, are the elements of the random force. The random force generates the fluctuations of returns we experience daily. A feature of a quantity generated by randomness, like a return, is that it can take positive, as well as negative changes. This fact will play a crucial role in our analysis of stock market returns over time, in the section, "Causality Dominates Randomness".

A forward step, and then a backward step of our portfolio return is a frustrating result from randomness that induces us investors to make investing mistakes. We seem unable to hold ourselves to do nothing, which in this case is the only appropriate thing to do.

Whatever we do to our portfolio arising from fluctuations in our return, we are in effect attempting to "correct" what does not need any correction. In fact, the net effect of our actions invariably leads to a decrease in our return, or underperformance with respect to our benchmark.

The Causal Force

The causal force equally drives portfolio return – only pushing the return up. The net-buy over a period is an element of the causal force. The motivation for the net-buy is the anticipation of share-price appreciation over the long term, based on the expected continuing growth of the economy worldwide. The continuing demand for goods and services, spurring innovations in science and technology, resulting in the creative destruction of old companies and their replacement by new companies – prods investors to buy shares of stocks. In the end, all these expectations depend on the continuing growth of the world population.

In other words, the ever-rising return curve ultimately depends on some form of Capitalism. In turn, Capitalism depends on human inventiveness and ingenuity for new ideas, in music, in the Arts, in science and technology. So long as human creativity flourishes, so does Capitalism, in one form or another, and so does the anticipation of share-price appreciation.

An important feature of the causal force is that its effect on the return has only the positive sign. This fact makes the big difference over the long time, as we will see below.

Let us examine the mechanics of how the net-buy or the net-sell arises in detail. At any instant when the exchanges are open, the market consists of a series of graduated offers to buy. In other words, say, Amy has an outstanding offer to buy 1,000 shares at $50. Beth offers to buy 2,000 shares at $49.875.

On the other hand, a similar set of graduated offers to sell is also going on at the same time. Cathy offers to sell 1,500 shares at $50.50. Dorothy offers to sell 1,000 shares at $50.75.

A sale only occurs when one side surrenders to the other side across this bid-ask divide, i.e. Amy agrees to buy 1,000 of Cathy's shares at $50.50. The other possibility is that a seller may surrender, instead, Cathy agreeing to sell 1,000 shares to Amy at $50.

When buyers collectively want large amounts of shares of a stock, they have to keep surrendering to successive layers of sellers up the curve. *The rise in price is a "net-buy".*

We note that the number of shares bought is always equal to the number of shares sold.

On the other hand, sellers who unload large numbers of shares move along the curve in the opposite direction; they have to keep surrendering to buyers down the curve. *The fall in price is a "net-sell".*

A net-buy may occur after a "surprise" positive earnings report. A net-sell may follow a bad news. To get an idea of the relative strength of price-rise to price-fall – in terms of the magnitude of rise to fall – we examine the long history of the stock market. We find that two-thirds of the time the market is positive. Thus, in the long term, the price-rise is greater in magnitude than the price-fall.

In other words, the net-buy is greater in magnitude than the net-sell over a long period.

To look at the notion of net-buy in another way is to look at returns, whether of a single stock or a group of stocks in a portfolio: a positive return means a net-buy; similarly, a negative return, a net-sell.

In resume, our portfolio return executes a composite motion, a return push up, or a return pull down, from randomness, and a return push up, from causality. The return push-up or return pull-down contributions from randomness do not grow in time due to cancellation; in contrast, the return push-up contributions from causality grow with time by accumulation.

This brings us to the argument for the case of causality winning over randomness, described in the next section.

Causality Dominates Randomness

Randomness and causality compete for dominance in influencing portfolio return. The change in return arising from randomness, as already noted, has two signs – positive and negative. In contrast, the change in return coming from causality has only the positive sign.

Thus, the cumulative sum of changes in return over a long time, arising from randomness, due to cancellation, does not grow with time and for all practical purposes is zero. However, the cumulative sum of changes in return, arising from causality, in the absence of cancellation, grows with time without limit.

Consequently, there must be a time when the return contribution from causality starts to pull away from that coming from randomness, growing our portfolio to the zone of unlimited growth.

As we indicated above, S&P 500 index return dataset points to 15 years as an estimate of time, from the start to take-off. With the take-off point established, our theory identifies two stages in the lifetime of a portfolio – *one, before-the-take-off stage, and two, the take-off-to-unlimited-growth stage until forever, as long as we maintain our portfolio.*

With the two-stage framework in the lifetime of our portfolio established, we can now think clearly about our investment in the stock market. We now have clear reference stages by which we can monitor our progress towards our goal of growing our money. We know at what stage we are in the investment process. In the rest of the book, we will detail what to expect at each stage, as well as what to do in the two stages.

Now, we are clear about what we aim for in investing – *portfolio take-off to unlimited growth,* riding the causal force, while sidestepping the random force, in the two stages in the lifetime of our portfolio.

This knowledge and understanding give us a sense of control over our investment in the stock market.

That is simple and clear as it can possibly be! However, is it as easy, as it is simple and clear? Unfortunately, the answer is, it is not – our human nature stands in our way, as we will see.

The Arrow and the Hoisting Crane

"Metaphors have a way of holding the most truth in the least space."
Orson Scott Card

"Metaphors are much more tenacious than facts."
Paul de Man

We now bring all the elements of our theory and their ramifications into focus with this metaphor: **the arrow and the hoisting crane.**

The metaphor provides an intuitive picture of the whole theory. The small arrow represents the effects of randomness on our return. The elevated hoisting crane represents tall structures – the ever-rising curve of our return coming from causality. A metaphor is easy to carry with us. It is ever ready to use anytime.

However, before we proceed, we need some definitions for clarity. Let the S&P 500-stock portfolio be the representative portfolio. Over a long period, our representative portfolio has a positive return. This means the net-buy is greater in magnitude than the net-sell.

Remember, the random force either pushes up or pulls down, while the causal force only pushes up. Some combinations of the composite motions of return are – a random return push-up and a causal return push-up, a random return pull-down and a causal return push-up.

Within a long period, say 20 years, any negative return in any year will cancel out a positive return in another year partly or completely. All negative returns and the corresponding positive returns that cancel out – all the buy-and-sell transactions that generated them, I define as **random**. Another way of saying this is that all the random return push-ups and all the random return pull-downs cancel out to zero, or average out to zero. A negative random return increment knocks down a positive random return increment – that is why there is no return build-up from the random force.

After the cancellation, all the positive returns that remain – all the buy-and-sell transactions that generated them, I define as **causal**. To put it another way, all the causal return push-ups add up to our portfolio return. A positive causal return increment adds on to a positive causal return increment – that is why the return builds up in the case of the causal force.

We keep these definitions of **random** and **causal** in mind as we move along.

A Sentiment Device

Imagine a small arrow with its pivot attached to a cable hung from a tall hoisting crane. The arrow rotates about its pivot. The hoisting crane slowly lifts or lowers the pivot, by winding or unwinding the cable in slow motion, as the whole device moves to the right with time.

The device mirrors the short-term and the long-term sentiments of investors.

The arrow stands for randomness. It rotates to point up or down at every random buy-and-sell transaction on stocks in the portfolio. In the push-and-pull language, pointing up is the random return push-up, pointing down is the random return pull-down.

It rotates like crazy—as many millions of times as the number of random buys or sells daily. The arrow has a built-in intelligence that computes the sum of return changes arising from the random transactions daily. At the end of a trading day, the arrow points either up or down, with length proportional to the return from the random transactions.

Over a long period, however, the return changes arising from the random force add up to zero. This fact is aptly reflected by the arrow – its furious rotation does not bring it anywhere; it merely rotates about its pivot, going nowhere.

What is the picture for the hoisting crane? We view the hoisting crane in two ways: the "integral" view or the bird's eye view – like the optimal path between two points; and the "differential" view or the detailed view – like the point-by-point changes in a curve.

The "Integral" View of the Hoisting Crane

The motion of the hoisting crane stands for causality – the causal return push-ups. Remember an element of the causal force is a net-buy over a period. Remember, too, the cumulative sum of the changes in return arising from randomness does not grow with time; the changes add up to zero over a long period. Furthermore, beyond the take-off point, the return is virtually from causality. The upshot of all these is that we can ignore the effect of randomness on the motion of the hoisting crane or the portfolio return, over a long period.

To drive home the point, we calibrate the motion of the hoisting crane in accord with the CAGR (compound annualized growth rate) for the whole period. By so doing, we are tracing the effective curve determined by the average growth rate for the period. We certainly can do the CAGR calculation for a whole period, after the period is over.

However, for the sake of argument, grant special powers to the computing unit in the hoisting crane to "smell" from the initial path the total path for the whole period. Then, the computing unit knows the initial and the final value of the portfolio, calculates the CAGR, and moves the pivot accordingly.

Thus, the curve traced by the pivot in the return-time space is a smooth curve – the effects of randomness drop out in the integral view– arching upwards along the return axis.

It is not outlandish to use the "integral" view. Nature seems to like it. Light, for example, seems to know (to "smell") the path that takes the optimal time. We know that light follows the path of least time.

Similarly, we grant the hoisting crane knows the effective CAGR right at the beginning, and calibrates its motion accordingly.

We move on to the detailed view of the hoisting crane – the conventional view.

The "Differential" View of the Hoisting Crane

The hoisting crane stands for causality modulated by randomness in real time – the causal return push-ups plus the random return push-ups or random return pull-downs – as exhibited by the running cumulative return. The "differential" view takes account of what happens at each point in time. The hoisting crane has a built-in intelligence that computes the running cumulative return based on information it gathers from the causal transactions and information passed on by the arrow from the random transactions.

Note the running cumulative return computed takes into account the compounding growth effect. Essentially, compounding comes from the fact that we roll forward the total amount—the original + the gains. We buy shares using the total amount. Therefore, when the crane computes the running cumulative return, it takes account of all shares bought by the initial amount plus all the gains at a point in time.

It hoists the pivot up or lowers it down according to the running cumulative return at the set time scale. At the same time, the crane moves the pivot to the right with time.

We set the parts of our device according to their natural time scale: the arrow we set in seconds, the hoisting crane in decades.

A typical scene is the following. On any trading day, we witness the arrow furiously rotating—to point up, or, to point down. However, the pivot hardly moves at all. The hoisting motion of the crane moves extremely slowly with its time scale set in decades. In a day, a week, a month, or a quarter – there is no perceptible motion. In a year, the crane moves the pivot a short distance. In a decade, the full stride of the motion of the hoisting crane is visible. The slow, if majestic motion of the hoisting crane, tells us it is foolish to act on the time scale of the arrow.

We should realize the stark contrast of the reality depicted by each component of our sentiment device. The snail-paced motion of the hoisting crane represents the running cumulative return. The squirrel-hurry rotation of the arrow corresponds to the random component motion of the return.

The enormous timescale difference between the two realities is a source of difficulties for many of us. One, we mistake one reality for the other. Two, our actions address the mask and not the reality behind the mask. Three, we assume that what we do to the arrow we do to the hoisting crane.

To the detriment of our portfolio, the arrow hijacks our attention. First, the time scale of the arrow is commensurate with our own time scale, ranging from a second to a day. Second, what the arrow reveals in the short-term return fluctuation is emotionally disturbing to us.

Unfortunately, for the reasons cited above, the arrow is the center of our emotional concern and attention.

On the other hand, due to its slow motion or its long time scale, many investors do not pay attention to the hoisting crane. Our time horizon is so short we find difficulty in taking a long-term view.

Summary

In resume, the dynamics of the two forces driving the stock market flow inevitably into a "time-point", when the random force wanes into insignificance, while the causal force waxes into dominance. At this point, we say that our portfolio takes-off to unlimited growth.

The metaphor of a small arrow hung from a tall hoisting crane is packed full of ideas, summarizing our theory of the stock market. The arrow stands for randomness; its rotational motion, though frenetic, brings the arrow nowhere – stands for zero contribution of randomness to return over time. The hoisting crane stands for causality; its tallness, the ever-rising curve of returns over a long time, requiring patience from investors.

The metaphor is also a "summary" guide to managing our portfolio – ignore the arrow, focus attention on the hoisting crane.

In effect, we have separated the random, the arrow, from the causal, the hoisting crane – in accord with our two-component theory of stock market return.

For a complementary picture of portfolio return, see the Appendix, "Visualizing Portfolio Return".

Chapter 2: Before Take-off

"The man with a new idea is a crank -- until the idea succeeds."
Mark Twain

With the background theory set, we move on to the elements of *investing for take-off*, together with the *go-with-the-flow psychology* – both ensuing from our theory.

Our goal in investing is to grow our money. We may view investing as a relationship triangle – of randomness, causality, and human nature. The relation between triangle members develops over time – specifically in the two stages in the lifetime of our portfolio. The three pairwise relations between members in the trinity are the subject of this chapter.

Before Take-off is the first in the two-stage lifetime of our portfolio. In this chapter, we examine the flow of the forces from the start until our portfolio takes-off; how the forces affect our psychology; and how the ancient Asian martial arts help us deal with the forces.

In particular, we will see how the return contributions from randomness and causality behave in this interval of time. Which of the two forces induces more errors among investors? Which inherited trait of human nature causes us the most trouble?

Our primary concern, however, is the flow of the two forces driving the stock market. How the two forces behave in time determines our attitude and our actions – what we should do and not do.

The Two Forces: Randomness and Causality

The behaviour of the two forces driving the stock market is markedly different in the two stages. In fact, the division of the total lifetime of a portfolio into the two stages is precisely coming from such distinct behaviour.

This section details the characteristics of the two forces, as their dynamics unfold, from the start to take-off.

In the stock market, the random force plays a negative role overall. It distracts us investors into actions that detract from our goal of growing our money. It lengthens portfolio take-off time – when a portfolio grows with time without limit. It plays to our weaknesses – for instance, our lack of intuitive understanding of random events. Indeed, we are poor intuitive statisticians. We suffer underperformance due to actions taken, based on mistaking statistical fluctuations for the reality of our return. Randomness may "ground" our underperforming portfolio forever, unable to take-off.

The causal force, on the other hand, plays a positive role. From the outset, it grows our money. In the absence of randomness, it shortens the take-off time of our portfolio. At any rate, it builds up its strength in the first stage, until it eventually out-muscles randomness in the second stage, when its percentage cumulative return is large enough so that no negative returns in the future when added can pull it down to a value below 100%. From that point onward, our return soars skyward – to the sky-is-the-limit.

The first stage is fraught with difficulties for us investors. The random force is equally as strong as the causal force at this stage. In fact, it can overwhelm the causal force, turning our cumulative portfolio return to be less than 100%. This means we are losing a fraction of our initial capital. However, the push upward by the causal force is present at all times. It restores the lost capital and some. In the initial years, the fortune of which force commands the heights can change many times. This can last to about 15 years or so.

Throughout the first stage in the lifetime of our portfolio, randomness and causality are at work establishing their dominance in the return. The signal characteristics of randomness are the erratic timing, the dual sign, and the magnitude of its contribution to return. Of the three signatures of randomness, the sign signature has the most telling effect on its overall behaviour over time. The sign of its contribution to return can be positive or negative. Because of this sign duality, the relative strength of its influence on portfolio return progressively diminishes into insignificance, from the start until the end of the first stage.

The above characteristics of the random force are equivalent to a time series of return contributions with random magnitudes and random sign of (+ or -). Over a long period, we expect the sum of the series goes to zero.

On the other hand, the signal characteristics of causality are its unpredictable timing, the singular sign, and the magnitude of its contribution to return. In contrast to the sign duality of randomness, the sign of its contribution is constant – positive – that determines its overall behaviour over time. Because of this sign constancy, the relative strength of its influence on portfolio return increases into dominance with time, from the start to the end of the first stage.

The above characteristics of the causal force are equivalent to a time series of return contributions with random magnitudes but with constant sign of (+). Over a long period, we expect the sum of the series to grow with time without limit.

Effectively, the difference between the random force and the causal force is the sign of their contribution to return. That is the distinguishing mark between the causal force and the random force.

Randomness gives us investors the most trouble. We have difficulty handling the fluctuations it throws at us. We specifically single out the negative fluctuations – the random return pull-downs. The positive ones from the random force – the random return push-ups, we do not mind – we do not even notice them.

The "red" numbers in our portfolio are a source of problems. They stir up our primal emotions and traits inherited from our ancestors – loss aversion, fear, greed, envy, herd mentality, poor intuitive statistician, and "hyper-causalitician". These traits pre-dispose us to make investing mistakes.

We will discuss these briefly in the next section. For a more detailed discussion on the role of human nature in stock investing, see our book, "IQ plus EQ: The Arrow and the Hoisting Crane".

Randomness and Human Nature

The key feature of randomness that provokes us to act on our portfolio is the negative fluctuation. The changes we do because of the provocation inevitably redound to the decrease in our portfolio return.

In the first stage, as already noted, the random force is equal in strength to the causal force. We cannot just dismiss it. The random force poses a real threat to our return; it could inflict harm to our portfolio, and not just psychological harm. We see it in our return, especially when we happen to open our brokerage account just about the years in a bear market.

For example, if we opened our account in 2000, two years before the 2002 bear market, we would feel no relief for three years of negative returns. We would know how it feels losing something like 40% of our capital! Although we knew that the loss was temporary – as long as we did not bail out – still we felt terribly then.

Admittedly, the random force also adds to our return by positive fluctuations – the random return push-ups; however, later it takes the addition away by a negative fluctuation – the random return pull-downs, or vice versa. "One hand giveth, the other taketh away". This advance one-step then retreat two-steps to say the least, is irritating.

The random force is an irresistible temptress to many of us investors to do something, anything to our portfolio to respond to negative fluctuations. It exploits the weaknesses of our human nature, by presenting opportunities to commit errors. We highlight our traits inherited from our ancestors that stand in the way to take-off below.

Evolution did not prepare us to be good investors. Eons of time sculpted us to be excellent at survival and reproduction. These skills do not translate into good investing skills. To survive and reproduce in the African savannahs, meant our ancestors were superb "causaliticians". For their lives depended on a quick and accurate discernment of an ominous signature from a benign one. This brings us to weakness 1.

Weakness 1: Our ultra-sensitivity to causes

The "red" numbers in our return, the negative fluctuations, prompt us to search for their cause. This search is automatic. It is the result of our ultra-sensitivity to intentional causes. Eons of history sculpted this tendency of automatic search for causes as a by-product of our evolutionary design for survival and reproduction. We can characterize our human nature as superb intuitive "causalitician", but poor intuitive statistician.

We feel uneasy if we do not search. However, we have no idea what it is. The following day our portfolio continues to be in "red". Our level of anxiety goes up. We become more edgy. The fact drives us to conjure up causes – any possible cause. Our emotions let our imagination range everywhere. We conjecture, say, our choice of our mutual fund manager was a mistake. Therefore, we decide to change mutual fund.

What is wrong with changing mutual fund, or any change in our portfolio in general? Many things are wrong with any change in our portfolio. One, it lowers our return, just opposite to the intended effect. Two, it costs money – the stockbroker's commission for every buy and sell, possibly taxes as well as opportunity costs. Three, change disrupts the build-up of increasing returns boosted by compound growth; instead, change fritters away the build-up opportunity. Four, it delays the take-off. Five, it can possibly "ground" our portfolio and never take-off. Six, either it indicates a lack of explicit investing approach, or it indicates a lack of seriousness with the investing approach chosen.

The low bar to making changes in our portfolio is abetted by our predilection to "idealize", as expressed by the saying, "Heard melodies are sweet, but unheard melodies are sweeter". Surely, we say to ourselves, the new mutual fund with a different manager will do better – only to find out that we have the same situation as before.

And the round of searching for a "cause" for a drop in return is on again. It is always on. The search for a reason or a cause for the fluctuation in our return is a search for a non-existing thing.

This tendency to search for causal agents for the negative events in our portfolio and to feel uneasy if we do not act on the perceived cause is partly responsible for the unnecessary buying and selling of stocks, or the changes in our portfolio.

On the issue of occurrence of random events, our sensitivity to causes is one side of the coin; the other side is our ignorance of the absence of causes. We are not only superb "causaliticians", but also at the same time very poor intuitive statistician. This brings us to weakness 2.

Weakness 2: Our ignorance of absence of causes

Over the eons, our ancestors did not learn an iota of statistical reasoning in the savannahs in Africa. Thus, we did not inherit an intuitive sense of the structure of random events – that random events by their nature have no "causes".

The random force presents us daily many "causeless" events that send us scrambling to find the cause. Our ignorance of the behaviour of random events finds its match in the random force hoodwinking us that our return is the fluctuation we see daily – this combination makes for a confused mind when confronting events in our portfolio.

Our lack of statistical intuition leads us to err in thinking that the negative return fluctuation has a "cause" open to our actions of stopping it. We are impatient to do something anything to restore our sense of control in what we regard as getting out of hand.

The statistical behavior of random events we have difficulty wrapping our minds around. The image of a hammer breaking an egg is absent in statistical events. One observation does not make a trend; neither, do a few observations.

We tend to act on the law of small numbers, i.e. we base our decision on one event or two. When a red number appears in our portfolio, we are concerned and may take action to replace the stock in question; or change investing approach; etc. If we wait long enough, to see more data points or long-term trends, we find that the "redness" and the "greenness" will come out in a wash, leaving us with the "real" thing, the returns coming from the causal force.

We intuitively feel that we will be amiss if we do not do anything. Together with overconfidence, this lack of statistical intuition is contributory to our tendency to keep "chasing heat"; abandon our investment approach too soon; and invest in and out of stocks.

All these partly arise from a lack of understanding of the nature of statistical behavior of events.

Let us suppose our brain wiring is such that we intuitively understand occurrences of events that exhibit statistical behavior. Further, let us suppose that our brain wiring is such that we see many events happen without a "cause"; we see events occurring but no "hammers"—in contrast to an egg breaking from a striking fork.

Then, the red numbers in our portfolio are no surprise. They are just fluctuations—a natural for quantities generated by random events, just like the portfolio return.

Further, let us suppose we learned in the savannahs in Africa that we could not control the statistical fluctuations in natural events, in contrast to some control we had with causal events. If we can identify the cause of an event, say a lion, then we can do something to stop the cause; options are open to us—kill it, run away from it, etc.

For quantities arising from random events, we do not even have the luxury of knowing the "cause", much less exercise some control. Then, we do not have to do "something" to neutralize the "cause" of the drop in our return. The drop is merely a statistical fluctuation we cannot control.

However, investors, in the hope to stop the perceived hemorrhaging of their portfolio, they do something—anything, instead of doing nothing. Most of the time, the right action is to do nothing. However, for the offspring of the African savannah dwellers, the hardest thing to do is precisely to do nothing.

It is inevitable that we suffer losses. Whether we like them or not, losses come and will keep coming. We all are bad losers. We hate to lose. We love to win. Our sadness for a loss is twice greater than our happiness for the same amount of gain. This brings us to weakness number 3.

Weakness 3: Our loss aversion

We hate to see the "red" numbers in our portfolio. Every time we opened our computer, we wished the screen showed green numbers. When red numbers showed instead, we were disappointed. This is our inherited trait called loss aversion. We suffer twice more from loss than we enjoy the same amount of gain. Alternately, our brain is willing to pay twice more to avoid the pain of loss as to enjoy the same amount of gain.

Our loss aversion makes us worry about our "winners". We hate to lose the gains our winners have accumulated. Because our mind is willing to pay twice more to avoid the pain of loss as to enjoy the same amount of gain, we sell our winners earlier. Using the commonly used phrase—*we want to lock our gains*. Avoidance of the pain of loss tips the balance against the joy of future gain.

Psychologically, we feel we do not have to acknowledge the loss until we sell our losers. Thus, to avoid the pain of owning up to a loss, we keep our losers longer.

As we have seen, randomness has the ability to stir up our primal emotions. One of the great motivators for action is the old emotion of envy. This brings us to weakness 4.

Weakness 4: Our emotion of envy

When we see the portfolio of others perform better than our own, we feel a loser. As we have just seen, we have an aversion to loss. We feel envy. We resolve to at least equal, if not surpass the performance of others.

Say, we opened an account with an online stockbroker. We religiously followed our portfolio. We kept tab of our returns. After three months, we were happy to have a return of 5%. However, when we learned our friend had a return of 8%, we felt a loser, envious of our friend. We began to doubt the "correctness" of our choice of stocks. We wanted to emulate our friend's portfolio.

If we carried out the emulation of our friend's portfolio, it was because we lacked an understanding of statistical fluctuations of returns. Over the period of interest, it just happened our friend was luckier than we were.

In the stock investing world, envy that sets us to follow others is a negative force. It is a force not for wealth creation, but for wealth destruction.

To emulate others' portfolio by abandoning our chosen approach is not good for our wealth. Switching investment approach before the return assessment time horizon (about three years) is over is not good for wealth creation.

Many of us may have seen the great Serengeti wildebeest annual migration on TV. Every year a vast number of wildebeests—a herd—timed to coincide with rainfall and grassland growth, gather together to search for fresh grazing and water. This brings us to weakness 5.

Weakness 5: Our herd mentality

When we see others loading up on shares, or selling their shares, we do the same thing too. It is difficult for us to be different from others. We feel the "protection" of the group when we join a group. This is the herd mentality, which we see in animal behaviour.

What is wrong with herd mentality? If we follow what others are doing, then it means that we do not have an investing approach, or that we do not take our investing approach seriously. If we do, then there is no room for copying what others are doing. We have our own way of doing stock investing.

Fear is one of the strongest emotions we experience. It is both a curse and a blessing. This brings us to weakness 6.

Weakness 6: Our emotion of fear

When the random force causes the stock market to plunge -25%, we sigh in pain as we see our gains in our portfolio quickly evaporate. The fear of losing all, as well as the pain beyond our tolerance to bear, is such that we lose perspective and push the panic button, dumping all our stocks to "salvage" some amount. This is the fear that springs us out of danger. This primal fear served our ancestors well when predators were stalking them in the savannahs in Africa. However, what was then a lifesaver is now a portfolio destroyer.

In stock investing, fear, in partnership with greed, plays a negative role—in a game of zero-sum. Investors with above average emotional intelligence or EQ gather the positive sum. On the other hand, those with below average EQ gather the negative sum. This is a way of describing the result of the wealth transfer from the "poor" to the super-rich in a bear market, where the fear of the "poor" exactly matches the greed of the super-rich – that is, when the "poor" are fearful is exactly the time when the super-rich are greedy.

When fear grips investors in the stock market, a stampede to the exits ensues, resulting in the free-fall of stock prices, sending tsunami waves across the stock market around the world—laying waste years of accumulated savings. The tsunami waves of fear would not be there, if mounds of shares at sky-high prices were not built-up by the other emotion of greed.

This brings us to weakness 7.

Weakness 7: Our emotion of greed

When we see others loading up on stocks, out of greed arising from the perception that the gains are for the picking and for us to gather as much as we possibly can, we too follow the herd maxing out on stocks near the height of a long bull run.

In the stock market, greed, in partnership with fear, figures in a game of zero-sum, as already noted in weakness 6 - fear. For one set of players, it is positive; for the other set, it is negative. The gain of one is the loss of the other. This is another way of saying what happens in a bear market: loss of the sellers is the gain of the buyers.

Greed is why many of us investors buy at bloated prices. Near the top of a long bull run, out of greed, we forget that there are dark clouds behind the stock euphoria. We pile up to buy shares at bloated prices. Valuation is no longer important. We load up our trucks full of shares of stocks. Unsuspecting the fall is imminent—we wax euphoric at the huge gains our portfolio has been racking up.

Then, a drop in the prices begins. We cannot believe it. We hold on. The stock market continues its decline. Out of fear, panic selling starts. Like in the 2007-2009 bear market, the decline can go to depths that we cannot take any more. Fear sets a massive sell-off.

Having gone through such "carnage", we vow never again to buy shares of stocks. But, it seems our memory is short. The pain of loss with time seems to fade. The stock market recovers and is on the way to a higher peak. Our instinct of greed gets the better of us with the rationale taken with great confidence that *this time is different.* True, the years are different. But, the forces at work—the *psychology* of people—are the same.

The results are predictable. The *boom* followed by *bust* is a cycle that occurs with clockwork regularity.

Causality and Human Nature

The characteristics of the causal force that affect human nature are its slowness in building its contribution to returns and its relative invisibility compared to the easily seen effects from the random force.

The two characteristics do not sit well with human nature's natural impatience. However impatient we may be, nevertheless, the flow dynamics of the causal force dictates its long-term build-up in overcoming the influence on our return arising from the random force.

The slowness of causality may induce the feeling that causality is not working. The wrong impression comes from the mask that return fluctuations foist on the incremental gains causality silently generates. In the short term, the gains it adds to our return are not obvious. However, over a long period, their accumulation could be enormous.

Compared to a day, a wait for about 15 years is like eternity. Nevertheless, we have no recourse but to wait. We cannot command the flow of forces to change according to our specification. This brings us to weakness 8.

Weakness 8: Our short-time horizon

We are pre-disposed to a short-term view. The daily alternation of night and day sets the natural rhythm in our lives. It nicely wrapped up the daily activities of our ancestors then, as well as it does our daily schedules now.

We investors are in a hurry to get rich. We want to grow our money the quickest possible way. The 15-year taxi time on the runway is incommensurably long for our short-time horizon. Investors, who are unaware of the 15-year time to take-off, and acting as if they can shorten the time to riches, will respond in various ways to the challenge of turning "red" to "green" that randomness throws at them.

Those who are aware, yet in spite of their knowing, they may ignore its implications and may act on the idea that they can shorten the time by beating randomness.

Go-with-the-Flow Psychology

In this final section, we apply the go-with-the-flow psychology of investing in the first stage in the lifetime of our portfolio. How do we address the investing issues arising from the dynamics of the two forces driving our portfolio during the first stage?

The key idea is to go with the force flows. We do not oppose the force flows, but use them, instead, to our advantage.

Dealing with the random force

We learned that the random force, in the first stage, is significant and contributes to return with a negative dynamics. In the short time, effectively it pulls down our return, instead of pushing it up. Being random, we do not have control over it. Nobody has.

In other words, negative fluctuations are inevitable. Moreover, nobody can time the market. In particular, nobody can time when a negative fluctuation comes, and thus, being able to avoid it.

Given this seemingly inflexible situation, what do we do? What should we do? Remember, "Do not meet force with force, but channel the force flow from your foe to throw your foe off-balance".

We throw the random force off-balance by not doing the expected response – that is by doing nothing in response to our return fluctuations. We do not meet the random force with our own force, by responding to a negative fluctuation, for instance, by selling offending stocks and replacing them. Instead, we sidestep the negative random force by doing the "unexpected" – doing nothing.

We do not do anything to our portfolio because one, it is a waste of our energy; two, it is costly; three, it lowers our return; four, it delays the take-off; five, it may permanently "ground" our portfolio; and six, the random force eventually becomes "toothless", only we have to wait for a long time.

Nobody can beat the random force! We weave our steps around it waiting for a vulnerability to open. Its vulnerability opens if we wait long enough – about 15 years.

To put it if differently, we do not do harm to our portfolio, by not doing anything to it. If we are able to do just nothing, then the slew of human nature weaknesses will be irrelevant to our portfolio. Human nature will no longer play a negative role in our investing.

Can we easily execute the go-with-the-flow psychology, described above – the injunction to do nothing? It certainly is not easy, by any means. The admonition not to do anything is a most difficult task for the offspring of the African savannah dwellers.

Our all too human nature stands in the way!

Our ultra-sensitivity to causes automatically executes the search for a cause for the "red" in our portfolio and presents us with an action plan and a directive to do it.

To the action directive, we have to say no.

Our lack of sensitivity to the absence of causes automatically searches for a cause even for random events. It prods us to do something. "Do not just stand there and do nothing. Do something, anything".

"Do something, anything" we have to say no.

Our loss aversion keeps badgering us of the certainty that our "winners" will lose their gains. Moreover, we avoid owning up to a loss by keeping our losers. Keeping our losers longer and selling our winners earlier are both bad for our portfolio return.

Keeping our losers longer and selling our winners earlier, we have to say no.

Our envy induces us to emulate the portfolio of our friend, which happened to perform better than our own. A voice in our head keeps urging us to emulate our friend.

Emulating our friend, we have to say no.

Our herd mentality induces us to follow others who follow others who follow others – no matter how silly the action can be, like joining a massive sell-off in a bear market.

The inducement to follow others, we have to say no.

Our fear of losing our hard-earned money makes us dump our stocks by selling at great loss, and by so doing, we are actually making the feared loss a reality. Our fear tugs at our heart to "salvage" our capital by joining the massive sell-off.

The selling we have to say no.

Our greed prods us to join a "herd" of investors to load up on stocks near the peak of the bull-run, thinking this time is different. Soon the selling frenzy replaces the buying frenzy.

To join the herd out of greed we have to say no.

Here, we are making some progress. Now, at least we are clear on what to do. However, it is not easy, given our human nature.

Dealing with the causal force

What is the disposition of causality in the first stage? It is fighting tooth and nail against randomness. Causality is the force that grows our money, the force that carries our portfolio across the long stretch of time of about 15 years to the take-off point.

The causal force is a positive force. We learned above that its slowness and its relative invisibility might tax our patience. In contrast with the random force, we can influence the causal force to some extent, as we will see in detail in chapter 4, "How best to ride the causal force".

In the psychology of go-with-the-flow, what should we do with respect to causality?

We should do all we can to ride the causal force optimally right from the start in the first stage. Here, we only briefly indicate what it is – choosing the stocks to populate our portfolio – as we will discuss it in detail in chapter 4.

We have to keep reminding ourselves, like a mantra, that investing is a long-time activity – at a minimum of 15 years, not a quick fix.

Impatience is most acute at the time of least information. It increasingly dissipates as we assimilate more information.

We have to allow "world enough and time" – about 15 years – for causality to establish its dominance over randomness, thereby reach the "Grail" of investing – portfolio take-off to unlimited growth.

Summary

The forces driving the stock market, randomness and causality, follow force flows, very different from our wishes. If we had our way, we would banish the random force; we would command the causal force to bring us quickly to the take-off point.

However, the natural course of the two driving forces prevails. Their flows are distinct in the two stages in the lifetime of our portfolio. In the first stage, the two forces are nearly even in their strengths, alternating which holds the upper hand.

The random force preys on our primal emotions, leading them to errors, by causing our return to fluctuate. On the other hand, the low visibility of causality's effects on our return makes us impatient, luring us to make changes in our portfolio. Thus, with goading from both forces, we flit from one fund manager after another, chasing the "hot" index or the "hot" portfolio, etc. – just to feel good that we are taking action nudging our return forward.

Moreover, the slow, long-time process in the build-up of our return arising from the causal force helps to divert our attention to return fluctuations. This attention often results in actions harmful to our portfolio.

The go-with-the-flow psychology of investing tells us to sidestep the random force, by doing nothing in response to fluctuations in our return. We let fluctuations be. The task is not easy to do. Our human weaknesses, if allowed to act, could harm our portfolio.

On the other hand, the new investing psychology tells us to focus our attention on how best to ride the causal force by choosing the stocks to include in our portfolio.

Our mind knows exactly what to do with respect to the two forces. However, our emotions may stand in our way. For our emotions to become a help rather than a hindrance, we have to re-program our mind via repetition. We will illustrate the way to do it in chapter 5, "Putting Theory into Practice."

In short, in the first stage, randomness and causality are about even in their fight for dominance in return contribution. Randomness, by causing our return to fluctuate, stirs up a "bundle" of emotions, impelling us to change our portfolio. On the other hand, causality – being slow in return build-up and having low visibility – tests our patience, prodding us to change our portfolio as well.

Going-with-the-flow psychology tells us to ignore the "red" numbers in our portfolio, and to ride the causal flow optimally. In other words, we ignore the arrow and pay attention to the hoisting crane.

Chapter 3: Take-off to Sky-is-the-Limit

"If at first, the idea is not absurd, then there is no hope for it".
Albert Einstein

This chapter continues the considerations in chapter 2 applied to the second stage in the lifetime of our portfolio. We trace the flow of the two forces; explore the interplay between the forces and human nature; and see how the go-with-the-flow psychology deal with the issues specific to the second stage. The inevitability of bear markets, as well as their effects on our psychology, deserves an explicit consideration.

We are now at the point when our portfolio starts its ascent to the sky-is-the-limit. We patiently waited for this stage for 15 long years. Now, take-off to unlimited growth is at hand. As with the first stage, the disposition of the two driving forces determines our attitude and our actions.

The Two Forces: Randomness and Causality

Randomness and causality continue to fight for dominance in influencing our return. At this point, we have been dealing with the two forces for about 15 years now. We know exactly what each force is capable of doing. We know exactly what to expect from the dynamics of each force, throughout the rest in the lifetime of our portfolio.

Below is a description of our expectation of the behaviour from the two forces, throughout the second stage.

Profile of the Random Force

Randomness goes on with its antics of negative returns, scaring us investors to take action, from the point of take-off to the time we decide to close our portfolio. It can engineer a massive sell-off via a bear market. Remember, by definition, any negative fluctuation is random.

Just like in the first stage, the cumulative sum of return changes coming from randomness does not grow with time and, over a long period, all add up to zero. Time does not improve its position vis-à-vis causality. In fact, time makes it worse. As we progress into the second stage, the random force is increasingly becoming irrelevant to our return, as the magnitude of our return increases.

Although the real power of randomness is diminishing with time – the power to affect our return, its psychological power is still formidable. Any sizable swing down in our return can send shivers down our spine, with many of us wondering whether a bear is coming, and thus, perhaps it is time to take evasive action.

A bear market, which the random force triggers, wreaks havoc to many portfolios, razing to waste a lifetime investment. This is true only for those who succumb to the psychological spell of a bear market. Except for its power on our psychology, randomness way into the second stage is a spent force.

Profile of the Causal Force

At the beginning of the second stage, causality is starting to outstrip the return contribution from randomness. The cumulative sum of return changes from causality is growing increasingly bigger, as well as growing increasingly faster. We are entering the zone of unlimited growth.

Its natural strength stems from its single-sign contribution to return, resulting in ever accumulating changes to an ever-increasing magnitude of our cumulative return, boosted by compound growth. Causality, in the second stage, so outpaces randomness in contribution to our return, that at a certain point no negative returns even bear market negative returns, can bring our cumulative return down to below 100%.

At this point, our portfolio has truly taken-off to soar into the zone of unlimited growth. If we properly maintain our portfolio, it will go on growing forever.

Randomness and Human Nature

In the second stage, as already noted, the random force is a spent force, with no real power to influence significantly our return. However, it still possesses residual powers opened by weaknesses in our psychology. We unknowingly concede and confer power to the random force. In effect, we are shooting ourselves in the foot.

To see this self-inflicted wound, we take the case of a bear market, which in our definition, arises from the random force. To make it more specific, let us say our portfolio's cumulative return is 500%. All of a sudden, a bear market of 2008 magnitude hits the stock market. This bear market yields a negative return of -36.6%, as in 2008 in the US stock market as measured by the S&P 500 index. Our calculation shows that -36.6% brings down our cumulative return from 500% to 317%. The bear market only makes a temporary dent in our return, which will grow right back to where it was and still higher.

However, psychologically, the picture is completely different – the economic world seems on the verge of collapsing. The drumbeat that this time is different we hear everywhere. We get the impression that the present situation is without precedent. It is very scary to be in a bear market the size of 2008. Our analysis above, though, is clear - it tells us not to worry. It does not permanently hurt our return; it just makes a temporary dent.

Nevertheless, our emotion, our psychology feels otherwise. Our fear of losing may overcome our logic, thereby surrendering our power to randomness. Many of us do, in fact, abandon our logic and yield to our primal emotions of fear, herd mentality, and loss aversion.

We join the fearful crowd in a mass sell-off, thereby conferring power to randomness, in spite of the fact that it has no longer any effective power over our return.

However, if we learned our lessons well, any action precipitated by randomness is detrimental to our portfolio. The more we are into the second stage the more randomness' influence on our return diminishes. It served us well in the first stage in ignoring randomness completely. It will serve us equally well to continue ignoring randomness in the second stage.

Causality and Human Nature

In the second stage, and way into it, the qualitative nature of the process of the growth of our return, of our money, changes. In the first stage, the growth of our return was approximately linear. The influence of the random force on the return pulled down what was an exponential curve to a linear one. With the influence on return from the random force progressively diminishing with time, the bulk of our return comes mainly from the causal force, greatly boosted by compound growth.

Way into the second stage, the curve of our return becomes exponential. To use the language of Physics, the exponential rise of the curve of neutron count means the system reaches a self-sustaining chain-reaction. In stock market language, the exponential rise of our return curve means our portfolio reaches a self-sustaining money-creation chain reaction – in principle creating money without limit.

As already described in the Prologue, a chain reaction is a process in which a trigger, like a neutron breaking up a nucleus of an atom, increases in number or in size at each succeeding phase, thereby producing a self-sustaining chain reaction – a runaway process. In the stock market, the "trigger" is the amount of money in our portfolio that increases with time, triggering or begetting more money as time progresses.

The challenge to investors, who reach way into the second stage, posed by the causal force is to understand the phenomenon of a self-sustaining chain-reaction, whether it is money creation, the fission reaction in an atomic bomb, or the fusion reaction in a hydrogen bomb and in stars. This is seeing similarities in things different.

To appreciate what is going on in our portfolio, let us take the time to see the details. Mathematically, exponential growth means the rate of growing is proportional to what is there available, in this case money. What is available – money – is growing. Therefore, this means that the rate of growth is growing proportional to what is available. In other words, the growth of our money is increasingly getting faster, or the rate of growth is increasing, or the growth of our money is accelerating with time.

The realization that the process operating in our portfolio is similar to the processes fuelling the stars in the heavens, including our Sun, to the processes in an atomic bomb – to say the least – is interesting. We now have an additional feature in our portfolio to look for and monitor – the attainment of self-sustaining criticality.

What do all these mean? It means that if we maintain our portfolio, our money continues to grow bigger, and, for some time will continue to grow faster and faster.

However, a time comes when the rate of growth will slow down. Infinity never becomes reality!

Causality no longer calls for patience as it did in the first stage. Instead, it calls for understanding to appreciate the processes involved in attaining self-sustaining criticality of money creation chain-reaction.

Bear Markets

Bear markets are inevitable. One of the pipe dreams of our books ("IQ plus EQ: The Arrow and the Hoisting Crane", "Portfolio Take-off: Stock Market Theory", and this book, "Investing for Take-off: Growth to Sky-is-the-Limit") is make bear markets vanish – perhaps it will remain a pipe dream. At any rate, it certainly will not be soon.

The fear of losing the enormous gains we are stacking up in the second stage pre-occupies our psychology. The worry shifts from return fluctuations in the first stage, to loss of gain accumulations in the second stage. The notion of "locking up" our gains, surfaces. The only way to "lock up" gains is to sell our stocks and park the proceeds in a CD or savings account, or in government bonds. By so doing, we stop the growth of our money.

However, are the above "safe" havens secure? All of them are subject to the risk of inflation. The best hedge against inflation is the growth of our money in the stock market.

Our minds think of security in opposition to growth. We think we cannot have both; it is either one or the other. In fact, the only "safe" haven for our money is the stock market – security from growth.

With a long time horizon, security and growth go together. In fact, security comes only from growth. With a long time horizon, the temporary dips or dimples in our return curve do not matter; they should not bother us. The average annual growth rate of stock returns far outstrips that of inflation. This may sound counter-intuitive; however, with a long-time horizon, the stock market is the safest haven to park our money.

The possible effect of bear markets on our return is so enormous that we devote the rest of this section to discussing the three actions we can take.

One, we see it coming and take the proper evasive action. This is true for a few individuals, like Ken Fisher, and even a veteran like him missed the last bear, but correctly sighted the previous three bears, as he claimed in his book, "The Only Three Questions That Count". For most of us, including the author, the skill is too complex to acquire. It is best to let the bear come, while we stay fully invested in stocks.

If we can sight a bear coming before it arrives, and we are right, then we have a huge leg up on the market. Remember the name of the game is to beat the market. If we turn out wrong, then we can be down big, instead.

To help assuage our feelings of being unable to escape a bear market, remember that the average return (CAGR) of the US stock market as indicated by the S&P 500 index was 9.6%, from 1928 to 2013. It includes all the 86 years in the period, including the 17 or so bear markets – small and huge, like the Great Depression bear market.

Thus, to stay invested in a bear market we act just like all the market indices. It is the normal thing to do. To evade it is out of the ordinary and requires the corresponding skill to pull the feat successfully.

Two, we join the mass sell-off, thereby losing much of the gains accumulated. Unfortunately, a great many of us succumbed to the temptations from the random force. Remember, any negative fluctuation is by our definition random. In chapter 5, "Putting Theory into Practice", we discuss a way to help overcome the temptation.

Three, we ignore the bear market – resting on the certainty that as night follows day, the stock market will recover. We stay fully invested in the stock market. In fact, if we have extra funds to invest, then bear markets are rare opportunities for loading on stocks. For, the whole stock market is like an Amazon store of stocks on fire sale!

Go-with-the-Flow Psychology

"How do we address the investing issues arising from the disposition of the forces, from our human nature in the second stage – using going-with-the-flow psychology"?

The guiding principle remains: we do not meet force with force, but channel the force flow to our advantage. In the second stage, randomness continues to do what it knows best – causes our return to fluctuate. In response, we continue to ignore the fluctuations completely. In other words, we ignore the arrow.

The harm that the random force can inflict on our portfolio, via our psychology, continues to be a concern. Bear markets are the occasions where these concerns can erupt. We will show a way of coping with these concerns in chapter 5, "Putting Theory into Practice".

On the other hand, causality markedly changed in the second stage compared to the first stage – its return contribution is piling up. On average, the annual gain of our portfolio is increasingly getting bigger and, if rolled forward, as already indicated above, attains a self-sustaining money-creation chain reaction – just like the sub-critical mass of fissile Uranium 238, if suddenly brought together, crosses the threshold of criticality, into a self-sustaining fission chain-reaction.

If we have a way of replenishing the spent fissionable material into the contraption, the chain reaction goes on forever. In like manner, if we maintain our portfolio, by periodically populating our portfolio with stocks using the investing approach we have chosen, the money-creation chain reaction continues.

Going-with-the-flow psychology tells us to continue riding the causal force in the second stage, as we did in the first. To put it differently, we continue to pay attention to the motion of the hoisting crane. The slow, long-time build-up is over; and, instead of low visibility, it is a high-profile money-creating machine.

Summary

The second stage transitions to a qualitatively different overall portfolio behaviour. The return curve behaves from a linear up-trending line to an exponential rise, just like the number of fission reactions in a fissile material reaching self-criticality; or, like a rabbit population exploding in number.

We continue to ignore the "antics" of the random force, or to ignore the arrow. Equally, we continue to ride the causal force or to pay attention to the hoisting crane. This time, the ride does bring us to the promised land of growth with time without limit.

Our portfolio takes-off. This is the "Grail" of investing! We should open champagne bottles to celebrate!

In short, the causal force wins, growing our money. Our psychology moves from worrying about return fluctuation, to worrying about gains accumulation – possibly losing them. Our portfolio ascends to the blue yonder, soaring to the sky-is-the-limit.

We move on to the next chapter to discuss the only positive action we do as investors, choosing the stocks or, "How best to ride the causal force".

Chapter 4: How Best to Ride the Causal Force

"Your theory is crazy, but it is not crazy enough to be true"
Niels Bohr

From theory in chapter 1, together with the discussions in chapter 2 and 3, the causal force carries us across a 15-year-time barrier to the threshold of take-off, and into the zone of unlimited growth. We also know that the random force contributes nothing to our return over the long term.

Thus, we will not have any discussion on the random force in this chapter. This is not to deny that it has a running effect on our return, but in the long term, its net effect is zero. Our understanding of randomness tells us to respond to it by doing "nothing". In contrast, the force we need to understand in order to use it best is the causal force.

Riding the causal force is like an eagle riding the force flow of air currents to stay soaring in the sky.

Thus, our aim in this chapter is to identify the driving factors of the causal force in order to ride its force flow optimally. In other words, what drives other investors to buy shares of stocks populating our portfolio is the focus of our discussion.

Populating our Portfolio

In a river flow, the speed of surface currents varies with position across the width of the stream. In and around the middle, the stream is fastest, with streams nearest the edges, the slowest.

To ride best the flow of the causal force, we have to identify the analogue of position across a stream in investing. The analogue is the choice of stocks populating our portfolio.

This is all we investors do positively; everything else we do is "avoid doing anything".

How do we choose the stocks? Postulate 4 of our theory asserts that *the causal component of return comes from the net-buy over the long term, by investors anticipating share-price appreciation, based on the expected continuing economic growth worldwide.*

The key word is *net-buy*. Over the long term, the net-buy pushes up our return. This means an overall net rise in the prices of stocks in our portfolio. Thus, we identify *price of shares of stocks* as a key driving factor, inducing other investors to buy shares of stocks in our portfolio. As buyers, we naturally seek the cheapest, everything else being equal. As sellers, we also naturally negotiate for the highest possible price.

This brings us to see what we can learn from a successful used-car dealer.

Graham's Principle of Margin of Safety

Success in stock investing is like success in a used car business. We have to know the price of used cars, buy them below their fair value, much less than their fair value – say, 50% or less. Then we sell the cars at fair value or near fair value and the difference is our profit. If we are able to do exactly as described, then surely we will succeed in our used car business.

This is exactly like investing. Investing is the business of buying shares of stocks below their fair value and selling them at or near their fair value. The analogy is more than meets the eye. The shares we buy are not "brand" new, like a brand new car. They are "used" shares, like used cars, in the sense that we buy shares from owners other than the company underlying the stock. Unless we buy shares from an IPO (initial public offering) from a new company, the shares we buy have passed around many hands.

As Greenblatt stressed, "If you do not know the price of a business, then you do not have any business buying the shares of the company". Knowing the price of a share of a company means we know the price of the whole business of the company. The price of one share multiplied by the number of shares is the price of the whole company. Knowing the price of the whole company means, we know the price of one share – the price of the company divided by the total number of shares.

To succeed in stock investing, we have to "pay a lot less" for shares of stocks. We have to buy "cheap", like 50% below their fair value. If, for any reason, something goes wrong, we have a margin of safety. Graham's principle of margin of safety is one of two perennial principles of sound investing.

If we buy companies with a margin of safety, i.e. at a price lower than their fair value—paying a lot less—on average, statistically speaking, the number of net buys, and the amount of each net-buy of stocks in our portfolio by other investors are greater than when we buy shares at or above their fair or intrinsic value.

There is greater demand on stocks perceived as priced below their fair value. The prices of said stocks rise by this mechanism. It may take time for other investors to see the situation as a bargain.

Mr Market and Stock Prices

How do opportunities like cheap stocks arise? Why do prices of companies go down below their fair value, thereby enabling us to apply the *first principle* of sound investing: the *"margin of safety"* principle? There are always stocks with prices that are unduly high, as well as unduly low, as Graham used to point out using Mr Market as a metaphor for the psychology of investors.

How is it so? When a company misses analysts' earnings estimate, which to begin with is at best questionable, investors tend to overreact. With our bias to loss aversion, as well as to fear, we tend to overreact to bad news. Investors who hold shares of the said company may dump their shares sending the price unduly down, much worse than what the fundamentals of the company underlying the stock truly reflect.

On the other hand, when a company for some reason receives much favorable attention from the press, and/or hyped reports, such as Microsoft in the making, or the next Apple; or the management runs the company extremely well, etc.—with our bias to believe and to greed, many of us form an exaggerated regard for the said company. We look at the company in much better light than what its fundamentals are saying. In our list of choices, we find ourselves ranking the said company as our first pick. Many of us will buy shares of the said company bidding the price unduly up.

Where does this lead us? To the conclusion, at any time: (1) there are unduly bid-down stocks, arising from our biases of fear and aversion to loss; (2) there are unduly bid-up stocks, due to our biases to believe exaggerated reports and to greed; and (3) we have to develop a method of finding out especially the unduly bid down stocks.

If we can find a systematic way of discovering the unduly bid-down stocks, then we can comply with the first principle—the margin of safety, or, paying a lot less. This means we will only have in our portfolio unduly bid-down stocks. We will be paying for them a lot less. We will have a margin of safety.

However, wait. Is an unduly bid-down stock or a cheap stock always undeserving of its low price? Do many unduly bid-down stocks not deserve the sentiment with which investors regard them?

Buffett's Principle

Beware buyer! Many cheap stocks are cheap because they deserve it. This brings us to the **second principle** of sound investing from Warren Buffett. He remarked buying companies at below average prices is good; but *buying good companies at below average prices is even better.*

Thus, we identify *good or quality business underlying the stock* as another driving factor, making our shares of stocks attractive to other investors.

If we buy good or quality companies at below average prices, then, on average, the same result above as for ordinary companies is statistically expected: the number of net-buys and the amount of each net-buy are greater compared to the case of buying at or above their intrinsic or fair value—even more so, compared with the previous case. Now, we have good or quality companies, instead of just ordinary companies, at prices below their fair value.

We expect on average, the demand for stocks is even greater for the case of good or quality companies than the case of ordinary companies.

Thus, the algorithm for our search is to look for unduly bid down stocks and choose the good companies among them; or, equally, look for good companies and choose only the unduly bid-down stocks among them. We will populate our portfolio, using this search formula.

At this point, we agree on the conceptual criteria for our choice of stocks/companies—cheap and good. We believe our criteria of cheap and good, i.e. good companies bought below fair value, enable us to ride the causal force optimally, thereby optimizing our returns—sending the hoisting motion of the crane up the most.

We now have to translate the concept of "cheap" and the concept of "good" into quantitative properties for convenient comparison to facilitate our search.

The specific translations of what is "cheap" and what is "good" spell out the different investing approaches. We will discuss one specific investing approach in some detail, the Greenblatt magic formula investing approach we use, in the next chapter, "Putting Theory into Practice". [For more details on the Greenblatt approach, see our book, "IQ plus EQ: The Arrow and the Hoisting Crane"].

Go-with-the-Flow Psychology

The go-with-the-flow psychology tells us to sidestep the random force, and not waste time and money to counter it. Invariably, if we do try, the result is negative – we incur cost, nerves, and decreased returns. On the other hand, the go-with-the-flow psychology tells us to ride the causal force optimally. This chapter focussed exactly on this optimal ride – the choice of stocks.

Selection of stocks depends on the investing approach we choose. Investing approach means two things. One, how we select the stocks, say using a discounted-cash-flow analysis or any method by which the stock universe narrows to a few that finally ends up in our portfolio. Two, how long we keep them, say for years or decades a la Phillip Fisher, or a Warren Buffett, or a year, or a combination of lengths of time.

Coca-Cola Inc., the giant maker of drinks, is an example of a company that we can hold for decades. It is not subject to technology obsolescence. Its share price goes up and down just like other stocks, but over a long period, it has an overall upward trajectory. This is the rationale for a buy-and-hold strategy for companies of this type.

Technology stocks, on the other hand, for instance Cisco Inc., have greater volatility in share price as well as in longevity. Thus, to hold tech stocks for decades may not be the appropriate strategy.

We will discuss in detail the investing approach we follow in how we choose stocks and how long we hold them, in chapter 5, "Putting Theory into Practice".

Summary

The continuing collective desire of all the stock market participants to grow their money is ultimately the source of the net-buy over the long term. We ride the net-buy, the causal force optimally by the choice of stocks populating our portfolio. Two principles guide our choice – one, Graham's margin of safety and two, Buffett's purchase of good companies at below average prices.

In short, buy cheap, everything else being equal, and buy good companies. In other words, we emulate grandma's patience in search of bargains when buying groceries and grandpa's diligence in search of quality used cars, not lemons.

The different viable approaches to stock investing have their different translations of "cheap" and "good" in the choice of stocks. I use the Greenblatt magic formula, which we will discuss in chapter 5, "Putting Theory into Practice".

Chapter 5: Putting Theory into Practice

"Ideas won't keep. Something must be done about them."
Alfred North Whitehead

"In theory, theory and practice are the same. In practice, they are not."
Albert Einstein

Generating new ideas is good, but putting new ideas into practice is even better. That is what we do in this chapter. We will be specific with enough details, from opening an account, to actually populating our portfolio, disarming fears of bear markets, retirement and home-grown dividends, to what we do in the two stages in the lifetime of our portfolio.

Passive and Active Investors

We have two kinds of investors – one, the passive investor and two, the active investor. For various reasons, the passive investor chooses not to pick stocks, or to manage a portfolio of stocks; opts to use the index mutual fund to participate in the benefits from stock investing, precisely instituted for the purpose. On the other hand, the active investor chooses to pick stocks and manage a portfolio of stocks.

At this point, we assume that you are ready to open an account, having acquired a working understanding of the theory.

Passive Investors: Mutual Funds

Passive investors further divide into the young and the old. The young ranges from a fresh college graduate who has a job, to one below 50 years old. The old is 50 and beyond. The young has time on their side, while the old has money on theirs. The young can overcome the handicap of a small start by starting early. The old can compensate for a late start by a bigger initial outlay. The old, if in normal health, has about 30 or more years remaining. That length of time is ideal for investing in stocks to grow money.

5,000	Table 1: Compound Growth			
Year	9.10%	11.80%	12.20%	16.10%
5	7,728	8,733	8,891	10,547
10	11,946	15,254	15,809	22,248
15	18,465	26,644	28,110	46,930
20	28,541	46,538	49,984	98,995
25	44,115	81,286	88,877	208,822
30	68,189	141,979	158,036	440,491
35	105,399	247,989	281,009	929,175
40	162,915	433,154	499,671	1,960,012
45	251,816	756,574	888,482	4,134,470
50	389,231	1,321,479	1,579,839	8,721,295

When we say the young has time on their side, we mean that even with a small amount of initial money, say, $5,000, it would balloon to a sizable amount over a long time, at rates expected on average of the different kinds of index mutual fund, as we see in Table 1. Note, the table is just a compound growth table – it is only that. Even if your portfolio has the average growth rate, its CAGR, say of 11.8%, the actual returns are not equal to 11.8% every year, but vary greatly from year to year.

With the caution duly recognized, after 40 years, by then the young turns 65, an initial amount of $5,000 would balloon to

a) $162,915 at 9.1% rate – a gain of $157,915

b) $433,154 at 11.8% rate – a gain of $428,154

c) $499,671 at 12.2% rate – a gain of $494,671

d) $1,960,012 at 16.1% rate – a gain of $1,955,012.

When we say the old can compensate for a late start by a bigger initial amount, Table 2 shows what we mean.

250,000	Table 2: Compound Growth			
Year	9.10%	11.80%	12.20%	16.10%
5	386,424	436,666	444,533	527,353
10	597,293	762,708	790,439	1,112,403
15	923,233	1,332,193	1,405,507	2,346,515
20	1,427,036	2,326,891	2,499,178	4,949,763
25	2,205,763	4,064,294	4,443,871	10,441,082
30	3,409,436	7,098,950	7,901,794	22,024,528
35	5,269,947	12,399,470	14,050,442	46,458,769
40	8,145,730	21,657,691	24,983,558	98,000,614
45	12,590,813	37,828,678	44,424,093	206,723,523
50	19,461,555	66,073,937	78,991,954	436,064,764

With a much bigger initial amount of $250,000 compared to $5,000, the gains are proportionally bigger – in this case by a factor of 50.

The Young

A practical consideration is the amount of money you set for investing in stocks. If you are young, who recently graduated and has a job, you probably depend on income to set aside a small amount to your brokerage account, regularly. In this case, a suitable way is to open an index mutual fund or ETF account. The initial amount required is affordable.

Funds fall into two kinds – active and passive or index fund. The actively managed mutual fund is one where the manager actively chooses the stock to include in the portfolio. In an index mutual fund, the market index the fund emulates sets the stocks to include in the fund portfolio. For instance, an index fund that emulates the S&P 500 index has exactly the same stocks as the index. I recommend index fund instead of the actively managed fund. The fact is that about 70% of actively managed funds do not beat the market, like the S&P 500 index. However, which index mutual fund?

In brief, index funds fall into four categories: one, market capitalization weighted; two, equally weighted; three, fundamentally weighted, and four, value-weighted. Market capitalization of a company is the price/share multiplied by the number of shares. Market-cap weighting is the allocation of funds to stocks composing a portfolio according to the ratio of the market capitalization of the company to the sum of market capitalizations of all companies in the portfolio.

Equally weighted is allocation of funds according to 1/n, where n is the number of companies in the portfolio. Fundamental weighting uses earnings or other economic variables, such as book value, related to economic size of a company. Say, we use earnings. The ratio of the earnings of a company to the sum of the earnings of all companies in the portfolio is the weight of the company in the allocation of funds.

Value-weighted is the allocation of funds according to the rank of a company based on, say, earnings yield (E/P or the inverse of P/E or PE), or the return on invested capital (ROIC), or a combination of both.

In a study by Greenblatt, cited in his book, "The Big Secret for the Small Investor", he showed that the market-cap weighted funds performed the lowest, followed by equally weighted, next the fundamentally weighted, and the best performer was the value-weighted.

We briefly go through the reason for the result just mentioned. In a market-cap weighted index, like the S&P 500, the index automatically reflects the price rise of a given stock because price is a factor in the weight of the stock. The higher the price rise, the bigger is the weight of the stock. A similar situation holds of a price fall of a given stock. The index automatically reflects the price fall of the stock. The lower the price falls, the lower is the weight of the stock.

It means that the index holds more of the unduly high-priced stocks and owns less of the unduly low-priced stocks. The market-cap weighted index doubles down on the distortions by Mr Market. This is the reason why market-cap index has the lowest performance of the four indices.

The equally weighted index does a bit better. To appreciate the improvement, the market-cap index systematically reflects the double distortion in the market by the very construction of the index. In the equal weighting, the market distortions are still present, but the index does not systematically reflect them. For this reason, we expect an improvement. Empirically, the improvement is 1% – 2% over the market-cap weighted index.

The fundamentally weighted index does a bit better still. The distortions are still present, but the index does not reflect them systematically. We expect a slight improvement over the equally weighted index because the variable used is more indicative of the economy. Empirically, the improvement over the equal weighting is less than 1%.

A big jump in improvement over the fundamental weighting occurs in the value-weighted index. To improve the performance of the market-cap weighted index is to own less of the unduly high-priced stocks and own more of the unduly low-priced stocks. The value-weighted index does one-step better than this – it owns only unduly low-priced stocks with underlying good companies. That is why the big jump in improvement. Empirically, the improvement over the fundamental weighting is about 4%.

In Greenblatt's website, valueweightedindex.com, he displays a graph showing average 20-year CAGR:

(a) 9.1%, S&P 500 total return, market-cap weighted,

(b) 11.8%, S&P 500 equal weight total return,

(c) 12.2%, FTSE RAFI 1000 index, fundamental weighting, and

(d) 16.1%, value weighted index.

It is obvious from the discussion above that the fund to choose is the value-weighted index. Greenblatt actually established mutual funds based on the value-weighted concept over a year ago. For some reason, his company transferred those who opened accounts in his value-weighted index to Gotham funds. Whereas in his formerly available funds, the entry amount was $5,000, now with the Gotham funds the minimum starting amount is $250,000. The high initial amount to open an account in Gotham funds may pose a problem.

Here is a way to circumvent the large initial amount, pointed out by Greenblatt in his book, "The Big Secret for a

Small Investor". The concept of value weighting is new. There are yet no funds established based on the idea, except briefly as indicated in the preceding paragraph. Nevertheless, investors can choose the best index funds available. After all, as indicated above, about 70% of actively managed funds do not beat the market, as measured by the S&P 500 index. Thus, if you invest even in a market-cap weighted index fund, you are still better than 70% of the actively managed funds. You can do even better than that if you choose from the list below.

Here is a list of possible candidate funds you can choose:

Equally Weighted ETF

1) Rydex S&P Equal Weight ETF (symbol: RSP)

Fundamentally Weighted ETF

2) PowerShares FTSE RAFI US 1000 (symbol: PRF)

Value Index ETFS (Not Value-Weighted)

3) iShares Russell 1000 Value Index Fund (symbol: IWD) – larger stocks

4) iShares Russell 2000 Value Index Fund (symbol: IWN) – smaller stocks

5) iShares Russell Midcap Value Index Fund (symbol: IWS)

6) iShares Russell Small Cap Value Index Fund (symbol: IJS)

7) Vanguard Value ETF (symbol: VTV)

8) Vanguard Midcap Value Index Fund (symbol: VOE)

9) Vanguard Small-Cap Value ETF (symbol: VBR)

International Value Index ETF

10) iShares MSCI EAFE Value Index Fund (symbol: EFV)

The Young and their Mutual Fund Account

What should be the attitude of a passive young investor toward the index fund portfolio? It must be one of confidence in the choice of the index fund. Once chosen, she continues to deposit an amount that is affordable, on a regular basis. She holds the account as long as she lives. She keeps invested all the time, recession, depression, or bear markets.

We will discuss in a later section, how to generate "home-grown dividends" for quarterly cash needs, in the words of Ken Fisher, in his book, "Debunkery".

The Old

The fifty and above have some savings but unsure where to put their hard-earned money. I started to invest in the stock market at age 51. My wife and I opened a Vanguard mutual fund account in 1998. The idea was to get started, and because of my personal skin in the game, my readings on the stock market had a strong motivation.

My wife's and my concern was losing our hard-earned money. The picture of a bear market was looming large in our minds. What are the odds of losing money in the stock market? The quick answer is the longer the holding time, the probability of losing money decreases to zero.

In particular, we do not lose money if we stay invested during a bear market. We do not bail out. We sit it out until the stock market recovers.

Say, you plan to hold your account in an index mutual fund for a year, then, the probability of losing money is 24/86 or 27.9%. This means that in four tries, you have slightly greater than one chance of losing some money. Thus, to invest in stocks for one year does not make sense. Those who go in and out of stocks for a year or so to time the market are up against Lady Luck.

What is the probability if we increase the time to three years? A way of answering the question is by a rolling-period calculation. For a three-year holding time, the probability of losing money is 15/84 or 17.9%. About one in six tries, you lose some money. Still, investing for three years does not make sense.

For a five-year holding time, the probability of losing money reduces to 11/82 or 13.4%. About one in seven tries, you lose some money. A ten-year holding time reduces the probability of losing money to 5/77 or 6.49%. About one in 15 tries, you lose money. At 15-year holding time, the probability of losing money is now 1/72 or 1.4%. In 72 tries, you have one chance of losing some money. For a 20-year holding period, the probability of losing money is 0/67 or 0.0%.

To interpret this zero probability is to say that for holding times longer than 20 years, the probability of losing money asymptotically approaches zero. A way to think about the zero asymptotic probability is to think about the probability of you crossing a street and a car hitting you. You would probably agree that the probability of that happening is almost zero but not quite zero. However, the "almost zero" probability does not prevent you from crossing the street to go to a grocery store.

If your time horizon is 20 years or more, and you have at least $250,000, then the fund that I strongly recommend is Gotham funds. The basic methodology for its stock selection is the combined ranking of earnings yield and return on invested capital. We will discuss this important topic in the section, "Greenblatt's combined ranking" below.

The Old and their Mutual Fund Account

As indicated above, I have a specific recommendation as to which fund to pick. My son has an account in Gotham funds. Initially, my son opened an account with the Greenblatt value-weighted mutual funds with the initial amount of $5,000, the minimum required. About six months later, the mutual fund clients including my son transferred to Gotham funds, as they were closing the value-weighted mutual funds. I suspect they were consolidating management.

The selection of stocks in Gotham funds is essentially the same as the Greenblatt combined ranking discussed below. The overall management of the fund is sophisticated. Gotham funds long the top-ranked stocks and short the bottom-ranked stocks. In other words, they buy shares of top-rank stocks (long the top-ranked stocks) and they sell shares of bottom-ranked stocks (short the bottom-ranked stocks).

The top-ranked stocks are below fair value. The expectation is that their prices will rise. Profits come from the rise in their prices and then you sell them at prices higher than you bought them. The bottom-ranked stocks are way above fair value. The expectation is that their prices will fall. Profits come from the fall in their prices and then you buy them back at prices lower than when you sold them.

If you have a sizable amount of money, is it wiser to buy shares of index funds in one big purchase or in several smaller purchases over time? Studies have shown that you are better off with a lump-sum purchase than many smaller purchases. With many purchases, your cost in commissions to the broker increases. Furthermore, you are better off invested than not, based on the fact that the stock market is up two thirds of the time.

The Young and the Old: Human Nature

The young may be quicker and the old may be wiser; however, in investing both are subject to the same weaknesses that humans are heir to.

How do both relate to the forces driving the stock market? Through the regular report by the index fund management, the two forces driving the stock market reach both the young and the old.

In the same way that the random force preys on the weaknesses of the active investor, the signature of the random force – the "red" return – stirs the emotions of both the young and the old, emotions of loss aversion, of fear, greed, the automatic search for a "cause", etc.

How do both relate to the causal force? The low visibility of return changes arising from the causal force subjects the young's patience to a test. Equally, the slow, long-time build-up of the return contributions from the causal force is an additional burden that tests the young's patience.

The old, on the other hand, may have learned patience over the years, but still the low visibility of return changes coming from the causal force may test the patience of the old just as well. Likewise, the slow build-up of return contributions from the causal force may add to the burden of the patience of the old.

The Young and the Old: Go-with-the-Flow Psychology

The go-with-the-flow psychology tells both young and old to sidestep the random force, that is, to ignore the return fluctuations completely, or to ignore the arrow. Moreover, the new psychology tells the young to add regularly to the account to improve the ride on the causal force by increasing the gains in their return, or increasing the rise of the hoisting crane. To the old, the new psychology tells them to ride best the causal force – a big lump-sum initial purchase than many smaller purchases over time is a way of riding the causal force optimally, or of setting the motion of the hoisting crane up the most.

In resume, to the young passive investor, continue to add to the initial amount in your account. To the old passive investor, starting with a big amount can make up for a late start. To both the young and the old, one, ignore "red" returns or fluctuations completely, or ignore the arrow; two, patience is a virtue that you cannot have enough; three, stick to your original mutual fund; and four, keep invested all the time, come what may.

Active Investor: Portfolio of Individual Stocks

Similarly, active investors divide into two groups, the young and the old. The young probably has to take a detour to accumulate money in a mutual fund. The method of stock selection I recommend that I use in my portfolio requires at least a minimum of $50,000 to $60,000 because you need to buy from 24 to 30 stocks in the portfolio. The old has no problem with the minimum cash requirement. When the young is ready with the cash, closes the mutual fund and opens an individual account for active investing.

The most important issue facing an active investor is choosing the stocks to populate the portfolio. In chapter 4, we saw that to ride the fastest portion of the stream, our choice of stocks to populate the portfolio is crucial.

Strictly speaking, to be able to make an intelligent selection, one needs to know the price of the business of the underlying company. The price of a business is the total stream of earnings in its lifetime, discounted appropriately for the time value of money. This is a most difficult thing to do.

Complications arise. One, the earnings are not constant; they vary over time. Two, earnings grow with the growth of the company; the earnings rate of growth is at most a guess. Three, one needs to determine what discount rate to use. The three complicating conditions make for a difficult valuation of a business of a company – even for an MBA. One can imagine the difficulty for an ordinary individual investor.

Greenblatt's combined ranking

A way to circumvent the valuation of businesses is to use the magic formula of Greenblatt. Greenblatt specifically developed it with the aim of enabling the individual investor to sidestep the difficult task of business valuation. It is simple to understand and easy to use. It comes with a corresponding website where the magic formula ranking of stocks is available, so far free.

In chapter 4, we saw that to ride best the causal force, we chose stocks based on two criteria: cheap shares and good or quality underlying company. Translated into searchable variables, "cheap" became earnings yield, E/P, or the inverse of price to earnings ratio, and "good" became the return on invested capital, ROIC. In the Greenblatt study, they ranked the universe of US stocks, about 3,500 stocks, in terms of earnings yield, from the highest, of rank 1 to the lowest of rank 3,500. The stock with the highest earnings yield was the cheapest. The ranking ordered stocks from the cheapest to the most expensive.

They ranked the same universe of stocks according to return on invested capital, from the highest, of rank 1 to the lowest of rank 3,500.

Then, they combined the rankings by the simple arithmetic addition. Say, company A had a rank of 1 in earnings yield but a rank of 450 in return on invested capital. Its combined ranking was 451. Say, company B had a rank 100 in earnings yield, but a rank of 2 in return on invested capital. Its combined ranking was 102.

The final combined ranking did not select stocks high in earnings yield, but low in return on invested capital. Nor, did it select stocks low on earnings yield, but high on return on invested capital. Instead, it selected stocks above average in earnings yield and above average in return on invested capital. The combined ranking – in the words of Greenblatt – picked above average companies at below average prices.

The result was "Goldilocks" stocks. They were neither too high nor too low in both rankings, but just right.

The portfolio construction suggested by Greenblatt is the following. Choose stocks from the top 24-30 stocks in the combined ranking. Allocate equal funds to each stock. Hold them for one year. Those stocks with negative return you sell a few days before one year is up for tax purposes. Those stocks with positive return you sell a few days after one year is up, for the same reason. Replace the sold stocks with the current top 24-30 stocks in the combined ranking.

He tested –back-tested the above scheme – his portfolio using a commercial dataset, from 1988 to 2004, a 17-year period. The performance was just spectacular! The CAGR for the 17-year period was 30.8%, compared to 12.4% of the S&P 500. The 30.8% average return beats Warren Buffett's 29% average return!

To appreciate better what these results mean, we translate the rates into money in our account. At 30.8% compound annual growth rate, $11,000 in your account in 1988 would become in 2004, $1,056,147 – more than a million in 17 years. The same starting amount would become only $80,245 at the 12.4% of the S&P 500.

The updated result, extending to 2009, remained outstanding: the magic formula yielded 23.8%, compared to 9.5% of the S&P 500.

Remember, these are average returns. It does not mean that every year, from 1988 to 2009, the magic formula portfolio yielded 23.8%. In some years, even consecutive years, it could have a lower return compared to S&P 500. This is a source of difficulty for many investors. When they encounter a patch, where the magic formula yields a lower return compared to the S&P 500, then they switch to a fund that emulates the S&P 500.

They are unable to think long term. They only see the immediate performance and not the long-term performance.

The method I use to populate my portfolio is the magic formula combined ranking. One, its performance is among the top. Two, it is available free so far. Three, it is simple to use and no emotion involved in the decision. Four, it gives the benefit of business valuation without the hassle. Five, the reach of the choice is deep – the top 30 US companies among 3,500.

For stock selection, I highly recommend the magic formula combined ranking.

In the heat of the moment, what holds you from dumping the magic formula is your understanding of the basis why it works.

Why the magic formula works

Why the magic formula works rests on two principles – the principle of buyer preference for low priced shares, as well as the principle of business success. Buyer preference for lower prices is easy to understand. It is part of our normal mind-set. The basis for business success is the golden-egg rule: the goose that lays the golden eggs outlives those that do not. A business that has lower return on invested capital eventually succumbs to the competition. In contrast, a business that has a higher return on invested capital flourishes, knocking down the competition.

Understanding these two principles will help you stick to the magic formula, under the heat of unexpected negative results.

Why the magic formula will continue to work

The magic formula will not become popular. This is the reason why it will continue to work. A widely popular method loses its edge because the stocks – the target of the method – quickly cease to be bargains.

Knowing human nature, many will take the magic formula for a trial ride for a year or so. When friends have higher returns than their magic formula's return, then, doubts begin to creep in. If in the succeeding year, friends again have higher returns than the return from the magic formula, then the magic disappears; what remains is a formula that does not work. They abandon the magic formula, endlessly chasing the "formula" in the moment.

Only those who understand the probabilistic long-term behaviour of portfolio return, and are convinced of the soundness of the basis of the magic formula combined ranking – only they will stick to the formula.

What is the significance of all these? The one chief obstacle – technical and not psychological – to success in stock investing is the valuation of businesses, the price to pay for a business. This is the cornerstone to succeed in the stock market. This is at the same time the Waterloo of many individual investors. Thus, the chief significance of this combined ranking in the magic formula is that the individual investor can cease to pretend doing valuation of businesses. We no longer go through the motion of business valuation. We just go to the website indicated below.

The Greenblatt rankings, updated daily, are available in www.magicformulainvesting.com.

Populating the Portfolio

This is how we populate our portfolio with stocks that put us in the midstream of the flow, riding the causal force optimally. We log on to the Greenblatt website indicated above and access the dataset drawn from 3,500 companies in the USA. You can choose any stock from the list. The recommendation, back-tested from 1988 to 2009, is to choose 24-30 stocks in the top 30. Allocate equal amount to each stock. The rankings are updated daily, an hour or so before the opening bell. So far, it is free. We hope it will remain so.

Remember that investing is a probabilities game, not a certainties game, nor a possibilities game. The 24-30 stocks protect us from the downside. At the same time, it limits us in the upside. We do not expect all of 24-30 stocks to yield positive returns in a year. Only about 60% of the stocks give a positive return.

We stagger the stock purchase/sale over the course of a year. About every two months, we choose four to five stocks from the Greenblatt list. At the end of the year, we will have in our portfolio 24-30 stocks. We hold them for a year. For tax purposes, we sell the losers a few days before one year is up; and we sell the winners a few days after one year is up. Every time we sell stocks, we replace them from the Greenblatt list.

We repeat the same steps of buying and selling of groups of four to five stocks every two months in the succeeding years.

What can be simpler than this? No emotions are involved. No weaknesses of human nature play any part. That is, if we follow the stipulations of the magic formula. A moronic EQ can still pull the plug, so to speak. An example of pulling the plug is fiddling when to sell. For instance, when we "feel" the stock has reached its fair value way before one year is up, we sell the stock for fear of losing the gains. By doing so, we have just allowed the entry of a weakness of human nature – loss aversion – into the investing process.

The magic formula insulates our portfolio from mistakes coming from our emotions. This is the most important practical aspect of the Greenblatt magic formula investing approach. With the magic formula, an individual investor beats professional money managers – 99% of them in my estimate.

First Stage: Taxi on the Runway

Just as in a real airplane, taxiing on the runway to take-off, the first stage in the lifetime of our portfolio is fraught with difficulties. With our portfolio populated with stocks, we start taxiing on the runway, which may take about 15 years. Our goal is to take-off at all cost. Our tactical goal is to shorten the taxi time.

During the taxi stage, the random force is equally strong in its influence on our return as the causal force is. Its negative fluctuation can be bigger than the positive return of our portfolio, sending our cumulative return below 100%. The first stage puts our statistical intuition to a severe test. Many of our problems in the first stage stem from a lack of intuitive understanding of random processes, and ramify to other weak traits like loss aversion, short-time horizon, herd mentality, fear and greed.

The most disturbing aspects of our portfolio are the "red" numbers. Before we know it, our loss aversion sets into motion a plan of action, say, change the mutual fund manager. This potential error arises because we are poor intuitive statistician.

If we intuitively know that the "red" numbers in our portfolio are just statistical fluctuations naturally arising from randomness, then we should do nothing to "correct" them.

Instead, we should expect fluctuations in our return. We should be surprized if there are no fluctuations in our return. In fact, a sure sign of fraud is a claim by any money manager that guaranties a fluctuation-free return, a 10-12% return year in and year out. The notorious Bernie Madoff made such a claim to his clients. Many, from small investors, to foundations, to people who ought to know better – all took the claim for the simple reason that they were ready – prepared over eons of history – to hear the claim. The Madoff claim is exactly how they want their investment to behave – to be without fluctuations.

It is not the real world. It is in the realm of fantasy. Madoff was successful in duping people because he offered them a fantasy world in conformity with their wishes, where returns are regular, steady, without surprises.

Back to reality, we emulate the way of one steeped in Asian martial arts in dealing with the random force. We dance around the random force in a waiting game, with the knowledge that it will eventually self-destruct in time. This means we completely ignore the fluctuations in our return.

What we do in the taxi stage – in fact, the only positive task we do – is to continue the re-population of our portfolio according to the investing approach we have chosen. If you adopt my recommendation to use the magic formula, then you re-populate your portfolio every year for about 15 years.

Second Stage: Take-off to Unlimited Growth

This is the "Grail" of investing – what we were aiming at all those 15 years of waiting during the first stage. At this point, the random force ought not to be a concern any longer. For, it can no longer harm our portfolio; all it can do now is to "carve" a dimple in our return curve that grows right back up, and even higher than the previous peak.

However, the random force remains a potential concern due to our psychology. It continues to prey on our fear, greed, loss aversion, herd mentality. Way into the second stage, our cumulative return, say, is now in the 1,000% range. Our constant concern now is the occurrence of a bear market. This concern is the aversion to loss of the gains accumulated and the fear of heights (our portfolio may be too high; we fear it is due to fall) – rolled into one. The concern becomes actual fear as the stock market starts to decline. We cannot believe it. We are in denial. However, the decline continues. Loss aversion kicks in.

We imagine our portfolio drained dry. As the decline continues, we no longer can take it – we join the herd and sell at a great loss.

We forget the long term. We only see clearly, what is immediately in front of us. We do not realize that the stock market always recovers and goes even higher than the previous peak.

Above is what we mean by potential concern due to our psychology.

In the second stage, we continue to ride the causal force by continuing to re-populate our portfolio with stocks according to the investing approach we have chosen. Using the magic formula approach, we do our re-population every year.

Is investing all this simple? Yes, investing is simple – one, if we use the magic formula, thereby avoiding the complex valuation of businesses, and two, if we follow the stipulations of the magic formula, without opening an entry point for our emotions.

Disarming Fears of Bear Markets

All our pretensions of rationality go out the window in a bear market. There is no clearer demonstration that we are not solely the product of Culture than a bear market. There is no clearer demonstration that we are the products of heredity than a bear market.

How do we view bear markets in general? In the first stage, bear markets delay portfolio take-off. They can pull down our return underwater. We consider them a nuisance. In the second stage, bear markets can no longer directly harm our return, but indirectly, they are still capable of doing great damage via our psychology.

Our theory tells us that way into the second stage the dominance of the causal force is so complete that no negative return – not even a bear market – can do any permanent harm to our return. Why, then, are we still concerned? It is because of human nature – a split between what we know and what we feel, a gap between our understanding and our emotions, a divide between our IQ and our EQ.

How do we heal the split and restore unity, connect the gap, or bridge the divide? We can join our head and our heart by educating our emotions through a re-programming of our mind. As we think, so we feel. As we feel, so we think. We use the former in re-programming our mind.

The core of mind re-programming is repetition of phrases or images. Countless repetition forms a habit. A habit produces instinctual action.

Let us work out a specific example: disarming our fear of bear markets. Our aim here is to transfer our intellectual understanding of a bear market as posing no threat to our return, to our emotions, i.e. the same understanding only now in terms of our emotions. It is important to know that our emotions make us decide and not our reason. Our reason presents pros and cons of an issue, but is non-committal. Our emotions, backed by reason, many times not, push us to action.

As we said, our aim is to disarm our fear. We cannot prevent the start of the fear emotion – that is automatic in the presence of a trigger. Nevertheless, we can prevent the succeeding phases – its build-up, and finally to action. We can disarm our fear from doing harm to our portfolio.

The aim of repetition of phrases and images is to soften the initial rejection of ideas on bear markets by our emotion, until their acceptance. How do we know the acceptance by emotions? We know the acceptance when we feel comfortable with the idea of bear markets as posing no threat to our return.

As long as we feel anxious when we think of bear markets, the acceptance by our emotions is yet to come.

The initial rejection comes from our inherited past – the loss aversion. We do not want to lose the gains in our portfolio.

Bear Market Mantras: Phrases

Our IQ (Intelligence Quotient) and our EQ (Emotion Quotient) often times do not share the same "view" on an issue. Our EQ's design was for codifying simple rules for survival and reproduction. A guesstimate is that 99% of its content is inheritance from eons of history. On the other hand, our IQ's design was for dealing with new and/or complex situations, with rules of logic embedded in its operations.

For *Homo sapiens,* investing is a completely new thing. It has no module in its emotion repository devoted to investing – like simple rules on what to do when stocks decline, as it has simple rules for dealing with snakes, for example. We are not equipped to deal with the stock market. Our IQ is the tool to use to understand the new situation – the stock market. That is what we have done so far in this book. That understanding – our IQ must pass to our EQ. This section attempts to illustrate how our IQ passes its understanding to our EQ.

Our IQ knows that a bear market, in the second stage, cannot do harm to our portfolio. Yet, our EQ feels otherwise. We now see why this conflict arises. Our EQ, the ever-watchful sentinel, sees a looming danger. The signs, our EQ sees, are the declining numbers in our portfolio, and that others are selling their shares. Our EQ rummaging through its repository of ready modules finds ones that apply closest to the situation: the fear, the loss aversion, and the herd mentality – modules ready to apply to the bear market situation.

What our IQ should do is to pass its understanding to our EQ, via repetition, in order to modify the action part of the modules so that we do not execute them. That is what we are doing in this section.

We have here a list of statements of thoughts, followed by a list of images that we repeat many times.

1) A bear market is only temporary.

2) My portfolio and the stock market will recover, and will reach a peak higher than the peak before the bear market.

3) Nobody can time the plunge or the recovery. For this reason, it is impossible to get out to evade the downside, and then to get in to profit from the upside.

4) To get out and in as suggested in (3) is the surest way to lose money.

5) The surest way to keep your money is not to bailout.

6) If you have extra cash, bear markets are the best times to load up on stocks.

Bear Market Mantras: Images

1) Bear markets can only "carve a temporary dimple" in my return curve, which grows right back up to greater heights.

2) Bailing out, in a bear market is like me jumping into the gaping mouth of a huge crocodile.

3) Bailing out, in a bear market is like me writing a check in the amount equal to my loss, to a billionaire like Warren Buffett, which will turn into cash when the stock market recovers.

4) Massive sell-off in a bear market is a massive wealth transfer from the poor to the rich.

5) Bailing out, in a bear market is like me handing my hard-earned money to billionaires like Warren Buffett.

Repeating these phrases and images until their acceptance by our emotions is the way to disarm our fear of bear markets, to disarm our aversion to the anticipated loss of money in a bear market.

Retirement

At retirement, when our regular income from employment stops, we begin to draw funds from our accounts. We assumed you opened an account for stock investment when you were young, or when you were old – 50 and above. Whichever it is, you should prepare for a-worst-case scenario – a bear market coinciding with your retirement.

Bear Markets at Retirement

We have just considered how to deal with bear markets in general. In this section, we added the special timing of a bear market coinciding with our retirement.

To answer the question what to do if a bear market coincides with our retirement, we have to make sure that six to seven years before our retirement year, we have sufficient emergency fund in CDs or savings account for our daily expenditures for about five years. This emergency fund can come from our savings, or partly from our brokerage account that by this time, six to seven years before retirement could be substantial.

With the five-year emergency fund set, we do not worry about a bear market because we can just sit it out until recovery.

Home-grown Dividends a la Ken Fisher

How do we manage our brokerage account in retirement? The idea is to have available cash to use for our daily needs, while maintaining our account to continue growing our money. We generate cash by selling the number of shares equivalent to our household expenditures for a quarter. For mutual fund investors, we redeem the number of shares equivalent to the amount of our quarterly expenditures. The cash is in our savings account before the quarter starts. We have three months to time the sale of shares or redemption of shares when the market is up.

We generate cash by this scheme, while maintaining our portfolio to keep it growing, as well as maintain our five-year emergency fund as long as we live.

Summary

Investing in the stock market is simple. Our goal is growing our money by achieving portfolio take-off to unlimited growth. To reach our goal, we take two actions – one for each of the two forces driving the stock market. One, we sidestep the negative random force. Two, we ride the positive causal force by the choice of stocks populating our portfolio. By so doing, we use the flow of the two forces to our advantage, thus achieving our goal of growing our money with the least expenditure of effort and resources.

The seeming perfect picture above, however, is not complete. Can we execute sidestepping the random force? Can we focus our attention on the ride, rather than on the "red" in our portfolio?

Unfortunately, for many of us, the answer is NO.

Our human nature stands in our way. The "red" in our portfolio automatically bothers us. There is no clearer demonstration of our inheritance over eons of history, than this simple automatic reaction.

How do we cope? The start of our emotions is automatic in the presence of a trigger– this we cannot prevent. What we can prevent, though, are the succeeding phases – the build-up until executions of concrete actions arising from our feelings. As indicated, a way to do this is by re-programming our mind.

With our re-programmed mind, we continue to "dread the red", but we do not do anything to "correct" it, thereby doing no harm to our portfolio.

Conclusion

"It is not rocket science"

Unknown

"Money never starts an idea. It is always the idea that starts the money".

Owen Laughlin

The difference between a rich person and an ordinary person is one of thought – the former believes he or she can grow money – with money begetting money, while the latter has not even thought about the possibility.

The stock market is an institution where money begets money. Ordinary people think only of working for money. They do not think of money working for them. The book shows a way of making your money – your hard-earned money – make more money for you.

The key idea in the book is that understanding the disposition of the two forces driving the stock market tells us what to do with our stock investment. With a robust method of choosing stocks settled, investing becomes essentially a waiting game – for about 15 years – for the random force to self-destruct into insignificance and for the causal force to rise to dominance. At this point, our portfolio takes-off to unlimited growth.

However, the clarity of our understanding does not necessarily translate into successful investing. Our emotions often derail our intentions. A divide separates our IQ and our EQ, owing to their different evolutionary function. EQ's design was for codifying simple rules for survival and reproduction, while IQ's design was for dealing with new and/or complex situations. As far as our EQ is concerned, investing is a completely new thing. EQ does not have any module in its repository for dealing with investing. It pulls out modules that apply closest in coping with a situation.

Thus, when a bear market comes, EQ draws out modules – the fear, the loss aversion, and the herd mentality – ready-to-use-modules that apply closest in coping with a bear market. We can align our EQ with our IQ to prevent our emotion from acting out the ready modules, thereby averting harm to our portfolio. We can do this by educating our EQ by re-programming our mind.

I hope this book helps in the cause of demystifying the stock market.

It is my conviction that we ordinary people can do the extraordinary things that rich people achieved, in terms of wealth creation.

As the common saying goes, "It is not rocket science".

Appendix

"Drawing is putting a line round an idea".
Henri Matisse

Visualizing Portfolio Return

Visual images aid our understanding. In particular, two agents or characters – the snail and the monkey – representing groups of processes help us visualize portfolio return.

The build-up of return arising from the causal force is a slow, long-time process. Thus, the slow-moving snail is a character apt to represent the build-up of the return component arising from the causal force. On the other hand, the combined processes of both random and causal force have a quick and a slow component, with the quick masking the slow. Consequently, the small-agile monkey is a character apt to represent the cumulative return arising from both the random and the causal force.

Both the snail and the monkey climb a vertical pole – their heights in the pole indicating our return. The height in the pole where the snail is indicates the cumulative return arising from the causal force. Similarly, the height in the pole where the monkey is indicates the cumulative return arising from both the random force and the causal force.

A linear scale, going up, with marks of percentages, starting at 100%, wraps around the pole. The snail is on the right side of the pole, the monkey, on the left. Both start at 100%, our initial capital – whatever is the amount. The snail can only climb up; once it reaches a point, it either stays put, or climbs up; it cannot climb down. The monkey has no such restriction. It can climb up, or down.

We now use the two characters to generate a visual picture of our portfolio return.

Say, year 1 was dismal – a negative return of -15%. The monkey, indicator of the cumulative return from both random and causal force, climbed down to 85%. The snail, indicator of the cumulative return of the causal force, stayed put at 100%. Year 2 was even more dismal – a negative return of -25%. A bear market hit the stock market. The monkey climbed down further to 63.75%. The snail stayed put at 100%.

Then, a recovery followed – a big rebound of 50%. The monkey climbed up to 95.625%. The snail stayed put at 100%. The succeeding year saw a smaller positive return of 10%. The monkey climbed up to 105.19%. The snail this time moved up to 105.19%.

By our definition, the positive return that remains, after the negative-positive return cancellation, is due to the causal force. After the cancellation, the positive residual of 5.19% is the running cumulative return coming from the causal force. Thus, the snail, indicator of the cumulative return from the causal force, moved up to 105.19%.

Let us consider a last scenario. The following year, a stock market "correction" occurred – a negative return of -8%. The monkey climbed down to 96.77%. The snail stayed put at 105.19%. Then, a positive year followed – a huge positive return of 36%. The monkey jumped up to 131.61%. The snail also moved up to 131.61%, a move of 26.42% from its 105.19% position.

The process described above is essentially the way we calculate the cumulative return. The added feature is the explicit showing of the one-directional motion of the causal force, hence its one-directional effect on return – upward. This one-directional upward motion is the reason why, over the long term, stock market return always rises.

The numbers used in our description come from standard calculation of cumulative return. The value added, however, comes from the visual part of our description. The visual part makes clear the cancellation of the positive and negative return components coming from the random force – to zero. Equally, the visual part makes clear the one-directional motion of the causal force, as represented by the snail, which either stays put at a point, or moves up.

The monkey is the indicator of the cumulative return contribution of both the random and the causal force. Seen over the long term, when the random contributions – positive and negative – cancel out, what remains is the contribution from the causal force; the random contributions add up to zero. Therefore, the cumulative return from the causal force is in fact the total portfolio return.

Notice that the monkey can only be as high as the snail. The monkey cannot go higher than the snail. This is because of the cancellation effect of the return contributions from the random force.

The climbing of the monkey follows the equation below:

Total = ∑Random (Push-Up – Pull-Down) + ∑Causal Push Up.

It consists of three terms – random push-up, random pull-down, and causal push-up. At the end of a long period, the random contributions cancel out.

Total = ~~∑Random (Push-Up – Pull-Down)~~ + ∑Causal Push Up.

However, while the period is in progress, the monkey can be climbing up and down – always below or up to the level of the snail. As we clearly see from the word equation, the cancellation of the random terms leaves only the causal push up in the return contribution.

On the other hand, the climbing of the snail follows the equation below:

Total = $\sum$Causal Push Up.

From the considerations above, we see that the monkey equation and the snail equation come to the same expression, $\sum$Causal Push Up, after the cancellation takes effect.

Thus, over a long period, the snail and the monkey come up to the same height in the pole. This means the random contributions – positive and negative – cancelled out to zero, thereby the monkey equation and the snail equation becomes identical: Total = $\sum$Causal Push Up.

The snail-monkey-climbing-a-pole picture is consistent with the metaphor of the arrow and the hoisting crane. Although both comparisons refer to the same reality – our portfolio return, each metaphor emphasizes a different aspect.

The snail-monkey-climbing-a-pole picture stresses the cancellation effect of the return contributions from the random force, leaving us with the clear result that our return comes solely from the causal force.

The arrow and the hoisting crane, on the other hand, highlight the enormous difference in timescales between return fluctuations and return accumulation in our portfolio.

Both pictures give a fuller view of our portfolio return.

About the Author

Feliciano Bantilan earned his AB Philosophy from St Francis Xavier Major Seminary, Davao City, Philippines. After his MS Physics from The University of the Philippines at Diliman, Quezon City, he went to the USA on fellowship to pursue a PhD in Physics. He obtained his PhD in Physics from Duke University in 1983. He returned to his country and taught Physics at the University of the Philippines at Los Banos.

Then, a bombshell dropped on his life: Parkinson's disease in 2002. The lowest point in his struggle with Parkinson's occurred in 2006, when his mobility was so impaired, he no longer could raise himself up on bed to sleep. He slept on a mattress spread on the floor. He would have episodes of near panic, due to difficulty breathing. Then, by a stroke of luck, still with severe movement difficulty--only a finger in his left hand could press keys of his laptop--he chanced upon the website of Dr Amy Yasko.

A year and three months into her protocol, he began to get back some of his mobility, as well as some of his "brain". In addition, something more: all of a sudden, he began to think in verse. He enjoyed reading and reciting poetry since he was young. However, he never composed a poem in his life, until his partial recovery. At age sixty-five, he began writing poetry. The first two poems he composed made up his first book published on September 20, 2013, *Einstein in Verse: Introduction to Special and General Relativity*. The rest formed the content of his second book published on April 8, 2014, *Life in Poetry: The Evolutionary 'Garden of Eden'*. He published his third book written this time in prose, *IQ plus EQ: The Arrow and the Hoisting Crane,* on June 10, 2014. His fourth book, *Portfolio*

Take-off: Stock Market Theory, he published on 1 October 2014. This is his fifth book, *Investing for Take-off: Growth to Sky-is-the-Limit.*

Other books by the author

Einstein in Verse: Introduction to Special and General Relativity

Life in Poetry: The Evolutionary "Garden of Eden"

IQ plus EQ: The Arrow and the Hoisting Crane

Portfolio Take-off: Stock Market Theory

www.ingramcontent.com/pod-product-compliance
Lightning Source LLC
Chambersburg PA
CBHW051812170526
45167CB00005B/1988